The Cult of the
Black Virgin

Ean Begg is a Jungian analyst and writer of guidebooks to the western mystery tradition. These include *Myth and Today's Consciousness* (Coventure, 1984) and, in collaboration with his wife, Deike, *On the Trail of Merlin* (Aquarian, 1991) and *In Search of the Holy Grail and the Precious Blood* (Thorsons, 1995). He read modern languages at Jesus College, Oxford, and holds the Diploma of the C. G. Jung Institute, Zurich.

The Cult of the Black Virgin

EAN BEGG

CHIRON PUBLICATIONS

WILMETTE, ILLINOIS

First published by Penguin Books 1985; reissued with new material 1996.

The moral right of the author has been asserted.

Library of Congress Cataloging-in-Publication data are available from the Library of Congress.

To Our Dear Lady of Einsiedeln,
Madonna of the Hermits in the Dark Forest,
with gratitude

Contents

Illustrations

Major shrines of the Black Virgin in Europe
usually accessible to the public

BELGIUM

Brussels, in Church of St. Catherine, *De Zwerte Lieve Vrouw.*

Hal/Halle, 29 km E of Brussels, in Church of St Martin, *Our Lady of Hal.*

Verviers, 20 km E of Liège, in Church of N-D des Recollets, *Mother of Mercy.*

Walcourt, 15 km S of Charleroi, in Basilique St Materne.

CROATIA

Marija Bistrica, 30 km N of Zagreb, *Mother of God of Bistrica.* Croatian National Shrine.

ENGLAND

Aylesford, Kent, England, 2 mls N of Maidstone, 2 Black Virgins in Carmelite Priory.

FRANCE

Aurillac, Cantal, in Church of the Cordeliers, *N-D des Neiges.*

Beaune, Burgundy, in Collégiale N-D de Beaune, *N-D de Beaune.*

Chartres Cathedral, 1) *N-D du Pilier,* 2) *N-D de Sous-Terre.*

Clermont-Ferrand, 1) In Basilica de N-D du Port, *N-D du Port.* 2) Cathedral. Behind high altar.

La Délivrande, 16 km N of Caen.

Dijon, Church of Notre Dame, *N-D de Bon-Espoir.* Now light wood.

Goult-Lumières, 22 km W of Apt, *N-D de Lumières.*

Guingamp, Côtes du Nord, *N-D de Bon Secours.* BV of Brittany.

Liesse, Aisne, 15 km NE of Laon, *N-D de Liesse.* BV of French Monarchy.

Limoux, Aude, to N of town on D104, *N-D de Marceille.*

Lyon, Fourvière Cathedral, 1) *N-D de Fourvière.* 2) *N-D de Bon Conseil.*

Marsat, Puy-de-Dôme, 3 km SW of Riom, *N-D de Marsat.*

Marseille, 1) In Basilica of St Victor, *N-D de la Confession.* 2) In Basilica of N-D de la Garde, *La Bouéno Méro Négro.*

Mauriac, Cantal, *N-D des Miracles.*

Mende, Lozère, 1) In Cathedral, *N-D de Mende.* 2) In niche above pump in Rue Notre Dame, *N-D de la Fontaine.*

Meymac, Corrèze, *N-D de Meymac.*

Moulins, Allier, in Cathedral, *N-D de Moulins.*

Myans, Savoie, 10 km SE of Chambéry, *N-D de Myans,* Queen of Savoy.

Orléans, Sanctuary of N-D des Miracles, *N-D des Miracles.*

Paris, 1) 35 Rue de Picpus, Chapel of Nuns of the Sacred Heart, *N-D de Paix.* 2) Neuilly, 52 Boulevard d'Argenson, Chapel of the Congregation of St Thomas of Villeneuve, *N-D de Bonne Délivrance, La Vierge Noire de Paris.*

Le Puy, Haute-Loire, in Cathedral, *N-D du Puy.*

Riom, Puy-de-Dome, *N-D du Marthuret.*

Rocamadour, Lot, *N-D de Rocamadour.*

Les-Saintes-Maries-de-la-Mer, Gard, black statue of *Sara the Egyptian.*

Thuir, Pyrénées-Orientales, *N-D de la Victoire.*

Thuret, Puy-de-Dôme, in Church of Initiates, *Vierge des Croisades.*

Toulouse, in Church of Daurade, *N-D La Noire or de la Daurade.* All that remains of the most famous site of the BV in Languedoc (see Solsona, Spain).

GERMANY

Altötting, 90 km E of Munich in Heiligen Kapelle, *Our Lady of Altötting.*

Cologne, 1) In Church of St Kolumba, *Madonna in the Ruins.* 2) In Church of St Maria in der Kupfergasse, *Mother of Mercy.*

Neukirchen beim Heiligenblut, Bavaria, near Czech frontier, 30 km E of Cham.

IRELAND

Dublin, in the Carmelite Church in Whitefriars St, *Our Lady of Dublin.*

ITALY

Loreto, 20 km SE of Ancona.

Oropa, 12 km NW of Biella, Santuario di Oropa, *Madonna d'Oropa.*

Tindari, Sicily, *La Madonna Nera.* Take the Falcone Exit on A 20 Motorway and follow the S 113.

LUXEMBURG, in Church of St Jean in the Lower Town, *Schwarze Mutter Gottes.*

POLAND

Czestochowa, in Basilica of Jasna Gora monastery (nearest

International airport: Cracow), *Black Madonna, Queen of Poland.* The most famous BV in the world.

SPAIN

Chipiona, Cádiz, in Franciscan Sanctuary, *Ntra Sra de la Regla.*

Covadonga, Asturias, in Picos de Europa, 10 km SW of Cangas de Onís, in Basilica of Our Lady of the Cave, *La Santina.* Spanish National shrine. Earlier paintings, including one in the official Guide, clearly show her as black.

Cuenca, Castilla La Mancha, in Church of St Antón, *Virgin of Light.*

Estella, Navarra, between Pamplona and Logroño, on road to Compostela, in Basilica, *Ntra Sra del Puy.*

Guadalupe, Cáceres, in Monastery Church, *La Virgen de Guadalupe.* Patroness of Extremadura and All the Spains. Her miraculous daughter is the Patroness of Mexico and All the Americas.

Jaén, Andalucia, 1) In Cathedral, *Virgen de la Cabeza.* 2) Church of St Ildefonso, *Ntra Sra de la Capilla.*

Jerez de la Frontera, Cádiz, In Church of La Merced, *Ntra Sra de la Merced.* Patroness of Jerez.

Lluc, Mallorca, 14 km N of Inca, in monastery church, *Ntra Sra de Lluc.*

Madrid, Julián Agarre 1, Madrid 17, in Church of Ntra Sra de Atocha, *Ntra Sra de Atocha.* Co-Patroness of Madrid, favourite of Royal Family.

Montserrat, Barcelona, in monastery church, *La Virgen de Montserrat, La Moreneta.* Patroness of Catalonia.

San Sebastián/Donostia, Guipuzcoa, in Basilica de Santa María, *Ntra Sra del Coro.* Patroness of the city.

Solsona, Lérida, in Cathedral, *La Mare de Deu del Claustre.* May give best impression of the original *La Daurade* in Toulouse.

Torreciudad, Huesca, 24 km N of Barbastro on N123 and A2211, *Ntra Sra de Torreciudad.* Where founder of Opus Dei was healed as a child.

Zaragoza, Aragón, in Cathedral of Ntra Sra del Pilar, *Virgin del Pilar.* Premier Marian Shrine in Spain.

SWITZERLAND

Einsiedeln, Schwyz, in Abbey Church of Benedictines, *Our Lady of the Hermits,* Swiss National Shrine.

Introduction

ARE THERE SUCH THINGS AS BLACK VIRGINS?

Oettingen for Bavaria,	Quod Bavaris Ottinga,
Hal for the Belgians,	Quod Belgis Hala,
Montserrat for Spain,	Quod Serra Montis Hesperiis,
Alba for the Magyars.	Quod Hungaris Regalis Alba,
For Italy Loreto,	Quodque Laurentum Italis,
But in France, Liesse	Laetitia Francis illud est,
Is their joy and ever shall be.	et erit suis.

This verse dating from 1629 catalogues some of the national shrines of Europe. At the heart of each is an ancient tradition of devotion to a statue of the Black Virgin. The poet could just as well have included Chartres, Le Puy and Rocamadour in France, Einsiedeln in Switzerland, Oropa in Piedmont, Our Lady of the Pillar in Zaragoza and Our Lady of Guadalupe and all the Spains. These are a few of the most famous among the scores of Black Virgins that have survived centuries of war and revolution, some in great basilicas, some in tiny village churches, others in museums and private collections.

If it is true that a large proportion of the ancient miraculous Madonnas of the world are black, why is such a surprising phenomenon so little known and what are the causes of it? Scholars are proverbially uninquisitive, especially about matters outside their own academic discipline, and the subject falls uneasily between art history and ecclesiology. To art historians many of the Black Virgins must appear crude, even grotesque, wormeaten, restored or replaced, of doubtful provenance, difficult to examine or date. Where they belong to a recognizable class, like the Thrones of Wisdom in Catalonia or the Auvergne, their dark colour has attracted little attention. The Black Virgin of Padua is well documented because it is by Donatello.

1. Montserrat (copy in Santiago de Compostela)

Theologians evince, if anything, even less enthusiasm for the subject than art historians. The still popular cult of wonder-working images is not only reactionary and non-scriptural, it also evokes memories of awkward subjects best left in obscurity like the pre-Christian origins of much in Christianity, the history of the Templars, Catharism and other heresies, and secrets concerning the Merovingian dynasty. So, blackness in statues of the Virgin tends to be ignored and, where admitted, is attributed to the effects of candle smoke, burial, immersion or fashion's passing whim. The contention, then, of the Catholic Church is that most such statues were not originally intended to be black, and only became so by accident later. The fact remains that they are black and to discuss the phenomenon in visual terms only is to disguise their deepest significance.

Over the last century, however, there has been an upsurge of literary and historical interest in Black Virgins, though this has largely been confined to France. Perhaps for this reason much prominence has been given to the twelfth-century origins of cult and statues. This has resulted in an arbitrary exclusion of many examples of the genre from consideration as genuine Black Virgin.

Since I am neither a historian nor a theologian and am no art expert, I shall be examining the subject from the viewpoint of archetypal psychology, treating legends and traditions as 'Just-So Stories' that are also of potential symbolic interest. I shall therefore not exclude from consideration a priori any site or image that has been associated with the cult of the Black Virgin.

From whatever viewpoint one examines the subject, however, and whatever the causes of the phenomenon may be, it is indisputable that some of the most famous statues of the Madonna in Western Europe have faces and hands that are black, by intention, and are known to have been so for many centuries. There are also approximately 450 images of the Virgin throughout the world, not counting those in Africa south of the Mediterranean littoral, which have been called black, dark, brown or grey.

SOURCES

The principal sources of information concerning Black Virgins are three general books on the subject, all of which confine themselves to France, with only brief references to images elsewhere. The first of these to appear was 'Etude sur l'origine des Vierges Noires' by Marie Durand-Lefèbvre in 1937. Her extensive catalogue includes paintings, copies of statues from outside France, such as those of Einsiedeln and Loreto, and several items listed on the basis of unchecked information from private sources which subsequent research has failed to verify. She gives, where available, a detailed and comprehensive bibliography for each entry. Her main hypothesis is the iconographical and cultic continuity between pagan goddesses and the Black Virgins.

This theme is taken up independently by Emile Saillens, who was able to avail himself of his predecessor's work, though his own researches began before 1937. His convincing and systematic book 'Nos Vierges Noires, leurs origines', which was not published, owing to the war, until 1945, contains a valuable catalogue of 'places in France that possess, or have possessed a statuette said to be of a Black Virgin' with a summary of information using abbreviations about each entry, as well as a number of useful maps.

Jacques Huynen in 'L'Enigme des Vierges Noires', 1972, although he owes much to Saillens, copying his list of images outside France verbatim, is particularly interested in the esoteric, initiatory aspects of the cult. This leads him to focus on the twelfth century, and the mysteries connected with alchemy and the Order of the Temple. In the second part of the book he examines in detail twelve French shrines and their symbolic significance.

The essay by Moss and Cappannari, 'In Quest of the Black Virgin', while informed by Saillens, is a precious introduction to the Black Virgins of Italy, and the fruit of a collaboration that lasted twenty years. Recent articles on the subject by Baigent and Leigh in 'The Unexplained' and by Brétigny and Sérénac in 'Nostra' have also been taken into consideration. Large numbers of locally published guide-books and brochures relating to individual shrines have proved to be mines of useful information. A predecessor to the present work from within the field of depth psychology is 'The Black Madonna of Einsiedeln: A Psychological Perspective', by Frederick R. Gustafson Jr. André Pertoka's cryptic monograph, 'Recherches sur le symbolisme des Vierges Noires, des dieux noirs, et des pierres-noires dans les traditions religieuses,' though suggestive, has proved, on the whole, too arbitrary and metaphysical for the purposes of this book. No. 266 of the journal Atlantis, Jan./Feb. 1972, 'Mystérieuses Vierges Noires' contains several articles with interesting insights.

Of the numerous works dealing with Marian shrines in general, I am particularly indebted to Fr J. E. Drochon's monumental 'Histoire illustrée des pélérinages français de la Très Sainte Vierge' of 1890, though in stating that of 1,200 remarkable French Madonnas, only 50 are black, he succumbs, I suspect, to the clerical tendency to minimize the phenomenon.

EVIDENCE FOR CONTINUITY OF THE
BLACK VIRGIN TRADITION

Early textual references to the blackness of images of the Virgin are rare, though Peter Comestor, the twelfth-century biblical scholar of Troyes and Paris, St Bernard of Clairvaux and Nicephorus Callixtus (1256–c1335), the Byzantine church historian, have been called as witnesses.

In a chronicle of the year 1255 it is written that St Louis, on his return from the Crusade, 'left in the country of Forez several images of Our Lady made and carved in wood of black colour which he had brought from the Levant'. The Virgin of Myans is referred to as 'La Noire' in a document of 1619, referring back to an incident of 1248. There is documentary evidence that the Virgin of Pézenas was black in 1340. Notre-Dame de Bon Espoir in Dijon is reported to have been black in 1591. The painting of 1676 in Bruges records the already ancient Spanish Black Virgin, Our Lady of Regula. Our Lady of Modène is known to have been black since 1623. The meticulous description and sketch of the Black Virgin of Le Puy given by Faujas de St Fons in 1778 is powerful evidence that the statuette was black by design, and had been so from its origins, which are no later than the twelfth century.

Even without historically verifiable examples there is an argument from common sense which merits consideration. Worshippers love the holy images familiar to them, regret their loss and resist any change in their appearance. This is attested by the ferocious revolts of the iconoclastic period in the Eastern Empire, as well as by the courage and tenacity with which local people strove to preserve their Madonnas during the wars of religion, the French Revolution and the Spanish Civil War. It is also noteworthy that Black Virgins, well-known as centres of pilgrimage in the past, lose much of their power to attract cultic enthusiasm once they have been painted over. That this fact was well appreciated by civil and ecclesiastical authorities is illustrated by the history of Our Lady of Einsiedeln. The statue was evacuated to Austria in 1798 to escape the designs of Napoleon. When the Madonna was returned in 1803, she was found, to the consternation of the Lords of the Capitol, to have been cleaned during her stay in Bludenz. It was promptly decided that she should be restored to her wonted blackness before being exposed once more to the gaze of the faithful. The copy of her in Fribourg was created black in 1690.

A further factor worth noting is the durability of local traditional names for objects, places and geographical features. We do not know when the Black Virgin, which has been the object of continuous veneration at Montserrat since the ninth century, though not necessarily in the same form, acquired her soubriquet of La Moreneta, nor when the Marseillais bestowed on one of their Virgins the title of La Bouéno Méro Négro, but such epithets as these, as well as the constantly recurring La Brune and La Noire, have a venerable ring to them and are unlikely to be of recent coinage.

Saillens estimates from the evidence that is available that by the middle of the sixteenth century, before the depredations of the Huguenots, there were 190 statuettes of the Black Virgin in France, mostly in the Auvergne, Bourbonnais, Pyrenees, Rhône, Provence and Savoy.

WHY IS SHE BLACK?

Spokesmen for the Church, when asked to explain the origin of Black Virgins, tend to invoke candle smoke or general exposure to the elements. After a time, they would say, as at Einsiedeln, the faithful become accustomed to a sooty image, and the clergy pander to their prejudice by the use of paint where necessary. Apart from the considerable contrary evidence of clerical antipathy to Black Virgins and disregard for parishioners' wishes, this rationalistic hypothesis raises two important questions. If the presumed polychrome faces and hands of the Virgin and Child have been blackened by the elements, why has their polychrome clothing not been similarly discoloured? Secondly, why has a similar process not occurred in the case of other venerated images?

There are, indeed, a few figures in addition to Mary and a handful of black Christs (e.g. St Flour, Mexico, Philippines, Lucca) who are occasionally represented as black. The other figures are interesting in that there seems to be a sound symbolic reason for blackness in their funerary, chthonic, sexual and occult associations. The list includes: St Anne, St Mary the Egyptian, The Queen of Sheba, Sara the Egyptian, St Catherine of Alexandria, the Libyan Sibyl, one of the Magi, the executioner of John the Baptist, St Maurice and his Theban legion, among whom Saillens includes St Ours and St Victor, whose cathedral houses the Black Virgin of Marseilles. The cult of St Martin de Porres is a recent one, but his image, improbably black for the son of a Spanish hidalgo and a South American Indian woman, has attracted a surprisingly strong devotion in the Dominican churches of Western Europe. Apart from Mary, however, black images are too rare to arouse much comment or controversy.

Black Virgins, on the other hand, are too widespread a phenomenon to escape curiosity, though until recently, this has been surprisingly muted. The aetiology that relies on exposure to the elements raises, as we have seen, as many problems as it solves, but there are other explanations, less current today than in the 1930s, both ingenious and disingenuous, which Saillens took time to refute.

1 Mary lived in a hot climate and would have been very sunburnt. The numerous portraits of her attributed to St Luke show this to be the case.

   Saillens points to the circularity of this argument. 'Why are the portraits brown?' 'Because Mary was brown.' 'How do we know?' 'Because of the portraits.'

2 Black Virgins were made by dark-skinned people of the Middle East in their own image.

   In fact there is no ancient tradition in Asia or Africa according to which Mary is represented as black. Even in Ethiopia she is generally shown as much lighter coloured than the majority of the indigenous population. Furthermore, Black Virgins, though often reputed to have been brought back from the Crusades, belong in most cases to the class of Auvergnat or Catalan Thrones of Wisdom and are considered to be of local workmanship.

3 The sculptors of Black Virgins naively supposed the inhabitants of Palestine to be dark-skinned.

   The reality is that contact between Western Europe and the Levant has been constant and considerable since 600BC, and the appearance of Jews and Saracens was perfectly familiar to the twelfth-century Frenchmen and Spaniards. A whole quarter of the city of Orléans (qv) was inhabited by Syrians from as early as the sixth century when the Irish missionary St Columbanus stayed with them, the Merovingian king, Gontran, being reputedly acclaimed by them in 588. The first Christian oratory in the Auvergne, dating from the fourth century was at Fontgièvre, near Clermont. The name 'fountain of Jews' refers, according to Pourrat, the foremost historian of the region, to Syrian Christians. From AD 768 to 900 Narbonne was actually a Jewish principality, and in the following centuries cross-fertilizing influences linking Islam, then in full occupation of Spain, with Judaism and Christianity, were particularly strong.

4 Prototypes of the Black Virgins were carved in black material such as ebony, basalt or metal, thus setting a precedent for future usage.

In fact, almost all Black Virgins are carved in wood, either of indigenous timber such as oak, apple, olive, pear, or in cedar. Ebony was virtually unknown in Western Europe until the thirteenth century.

CHRISTIAN ATTITUDES TO THE BLACK VIRGIN CULT

Many Christians, both among the clergy and the laity, simply accept that the Black Virgins present us with a mystery for which there is no obvious explanation. In 1944, Leonard W. Moss, entering the church at Lucera in southern Italy, came across his first Black Virgin and asked the priest, 'Father, why is the Madonna black?' The response was, 'My son, she is black because she is black.' When, in December 1980, I visited Orcival, whose wonder-working Madonna figures in all the lists of Black Virgins, though her appearance belies the description, I asked the proprietress of the souvenir shop opposite the church why she was called black. The answer, in a tone which brooked no further cross-examination, was 'Because she is.'

The priest's answer to Moss may seem a charming example of holy simplicity, but there was no mistaking the open hostility, when, on 28 December 1952, as Moss and Cappannari presented their paper on Black Virgins to the American

Association for the Advancement of Science, every priest and nun in the audience walked out. My impression of the reaction of the clergy to the subject of Black Virgins has been one of helpful courtesy tinged with genuine disinterest in and ignorance of the subject. As a result, many cults are dying.

At Ballon near Le Mans, one of the many places in France that echo the name of Belenus, the Celtic god of flocks, and its suggestively named twin parish of St Mars-sous-Ballon, the priest knew nothing of any cult of the Virgin, black or otherwise, in the neighbourhood. None of the local inhabitants I spoke to could recall any particular Marian devotion. Yet Saillens writes categorically of the fifteenth-century Notre-Dame des Champs at Ballon as the only example of an earthenware Black Virgin in France, and states that it is now in a private collection, having been replaced in the nineteenth century at St Mars by a standing wooden statue of 150cm.

At Bollène (another Belenus town?) on the southern Rhône, in more typical Black Virgin country, and its neighbouring parish of Mondragon, six kilometres away, with the chapel of St Aries half way between them, another agricultural Madonna; Notre-Dame des Plans, is vouched for as black by Drochon, Durand-Lefèbvre and Saillens, all giving somewhat different information about it. The parish priest, who was again helpful and friendly, showed me the ancient and famous statue of the Virgin and Child, with carved draperies in red, and natural complexions with no trace of blackness. He had never heard it called a Black Virgin.

Our Lady of the Hollies at Arfeuilles, a druidic centre, is also noted as black, ancient and interesting by all three authors as at Bollène. Drochon writes of the statue: 'One of the most interesting images which Christian art has bequeathed to us, she was formerly completely black.' Regretting that she had been whitened in the middle of the nineteenth century, he adds, though he has no special interest in Black Virgins: 'God preserve our churches from these ill-advised restorers.' When I visited the church in 1980, the elderly woman sacristan knew nothing of any Black Virgin, but remembered the statue, which was badly worm-eaten, being taken away in 1938 and returning refurbished, repainted and gilded. The same fate overtook Our Lady of the Thornbush, or of Life, at Avioth near the Belgian frontier, which had certainly been black at one time. Like her sister of Arfeuilles, she specialized in resuscitating dead babies so that they might be baptised and gain admission to heaven, and, as at Arfeuilles, the cult seems diminished since her blackness was purged. At Dijon I was told by a newsagent that the priest will not permit the sale of postcards of Our Lady of Good Hope, one of the most famous and ancient of French Black Virgins, though now considerably paler than of yore.

These few examples, among many, of clerical opposition to Black Virgins leading to diminution of fervour, are in sharp contrast to the almost ferocious exclusiveness with which the faithful in some communities guard the secret of their, still black, Madonnas. The curator of the castle museum at Le Barroux who held the key to the hill-top chapel where the local Black Virgin was reputed to be situated, rudely refused both the key and any information as to the image's whereabouts. The remarkable Black Virgin of Belloc has been transferred from her abandoned mountain sanctuary to the village church of Dorres. The proprietress of the adjacent hotel who holds the key said the church was now never opened under any circumstances, except during Mass, which was not a frequent occurrence as the priest had to serve five parishes and a large mental hospital. It may be that the theft of the Black Virgin of Nuria, the most famous of the Pyrenees and only a few miles across the frontier, and that of the ancient Madonna of St Martin du Canigou, has helped to fan the flames of suspicious protectiveness throughout the region.

Few original statues are left in isolated chapels these days, in which a growing epidemic of thefts is proving the greatest scourge of Black Virgins since the French Revolution, and, when they are still in existence, the sanctuaries are firmly sealed against anyone seeking entrance or even a glimpse of the interior. Our Lady of the Oak-Tree on the Col d'Arès near Prats-de-Mollo has been removed from public veneration to the safe-keeping of the presbytery, as has La Belle Briançonne, removed from the chapel of St Etienne-des-Grès near Tarascon. Even famous statues in the middle of towns are not immune to eclipse. At Manosque, in Provence, home of Our Lady of the Brambles and of Life, whom Durand-Lefèbvre describes as 'the doyenne of our Black Virgins', and to whom Huynen brought renewed publicity when he consecrated a whole chapter of his book to her, the church has been closed for some years for repairs and no one seemed to know either when it would reopen or where the famous image could be seen. There were no postcards or photographs of it on sale in the town, and no local guide-books referring to it. It seemed as though Manosque's most celebrated inhabitant was already half forgotten, while the local authorities write that she is hidden and may not be seen. Some 30 miles away, in contrast, at the other end of the Lubéron range, the little Santo Vierge Négro of Goult-Lumières, who outshines as a wonder-worker the more flamboyant Lady of Light on the high altar, has been replaced by a copy since her theft in 1978, but continues to attract a fervent following, thanks to the devoted work of the nuns who keep the pilgrimage centre.

It seems then that a remarkable cultural survival of great mystery and antiquity is ironically in danger of disappearing from all but a few well-protected sites just at the moment when the attention of a wider public is being directed towards it. The Black Virgins of France that survived the fury of the Huguenots and the Revolutionaries are now being subjected to a three-fold process of attrition from thefts of uncertain motivation, the indifference and neglect of a sceptical age, and embarrassed suppression by the Church, often disguised as protectiveness. Why should the Church feel so sensitive about its Black Virgins?

The cult has inevitably suffered since the Second Vatican Council from the prevailing animus against 'non-historical orthodoxy' and in favour of biblical truth and simplicity of worship. But another reason for clerical lack of enthusiasm when faced with the enduring popularity of the Black Virgins may owe something, not merely to liturgical trends, but to suspicion of the sort of people who are attracted by the phenomenon. Joan of Arc, now raised to the altars, and safely dead for five and a half centuries, was not in her lifetime a favourite daughter of the Church, though her special devotion to Black Virgins would not have been viewed askance in her day. More recent devotees have, however, included the writers, Anatole France, noted for his mocking and ironical wit, often at the expense of orthodox religion, and J.-K. Huysmans, frequenter of magicians, who, before his conversion was notorious for his tales of debauchery and occultism including his sensational description of a black mass. Neither of these nor the elusive alchemist, Fulcanelli, author of *Le Mystère des Cathédrales*, are the sort of people calculated to allay clerical hesitancy towards Black Virgin fanciers, but there have been other examples which are even less reassuring.

Not far from Domrémy, birth-place of Joan of Arc, there rises from the plateau an impressive 500 metre high table mountain with a blunt peak at either end, whose name, Sion-Vaudémont, fortuitously links the mountain of the Lord to that of Wotan. Huynen states that, from the Middle Ages to the Revolution, a Black Virgin reigned there, though which of the various statues associated with the shrine he is referring to is not clear. What is certain is that Sion, 'La Colline Inspirée' of Barrès, has had an eventful history since St Gérard of Toul placed a statue of Mary on the mountain in 994, in place of pagan Rosmerta. Through the vicissitudes of life in a frontier province, Our Lady of Sion has remained the tutelary patroness of Lorraine.

A piquant page of the mountain's history involves one of the great religious scandals of the nineteenth century. In 1838 the three brothers Baillard, all priests, more or less simultaneously established houses of a new Catholic religious order, the Brothers of Christian Doctrine, on the two holy mountains of Alsace and Lorraine, Mount St Odile and Sion, which they had somehow managed to acquire. From 1843 they fell under the spell of a magus and mystagogue known variously as Michel Vintras, the French Jeremiah, Elias the Artist and the Organ. Vintras preached the advent of the Age of the Holy Spirit, long prophesied by Joachim of Flora, which would coincide with a redemption wrought by the Virgin Mediatrix and her pre-destined priestesses. In this new dispensation the greatest sacrament was the sexual act, through which the original androgyny would be restored. Thus, on the mountain of Rosmerta, the love-goddess, the sacred prostitution of the old high places and the orgiastic communion of licentious Gnostics were celebrated anew. Another devotion was that to Joan of Arc, the star pointing the way to the Marian dawn, the salvific one who would introduce the great monarch, the lily whose mission was to unite herself in love with the greatest of the saints. Despite international support and interest, which included apparently, that of the House of Habsburg, bishops and police had their way, and with the suppression in 1852 of the Baillard establishment, the great experiment came to an end. During excavations that took place towards the end of the century, a bronze statuette of a hermaphrodite, well endowed with both sexual characteristics, was unearthed at Sion and placed in a museum in Nancy where it so scandalized the conventions of the period that it had to be withdrawn from public view.

Even without the assistance of the Baillard brothers and their successors, the attention of a rational and progressive age is being directed towards the archetypal feminine. Strange things do happen. For example, between 1928 and 1972, 232 apparitions of the Virgin attracted sufficient interest to be reported in the press and be investigated by the Church authorities. Since 1972 many more apparitions as well as statues of the Virgin that weep and move have been reported. As recently as 1982 and 1983 a pagan Black Virgin made according to ancient rites was venerated in the course of Druidic ceremonies at St Georges Nigremont. So, perhaps, despite the countervailing spirit of the age it is too early to close the chapter of odd events connected with the cult of the Virgin. But apart from those supernatural interventions in favour of the Marian cult in general, the story of the Black Virgin may also include a heretical secret with the power to shock and astonish even current post-Christian attitudes, a secret, moreover, closely involving political forces still influential in modern Europe. Small wonder if the Church's public attitude to the subject is one of extreme caution.

THE PRIEURÉ DE SION AND THE BLACK VIRGIN

That early images of the Madonna and Child were based on those of Isis and Horus is generally accepted. That the cult of the Black Virgin is essentially a product of the twelfth-century Gothic renaissance, which was a period of religious novelty as well as of faith, is also well established. The legendary origin of so many of the statuettes in the baggage trains of returning crusaders, especially when they happened to be Templars, is no guarantee of the orthodoxy of their cult. That many legends of the period connect the twelfth-century Black Virgins with an earlier miraculous origin dating from the Merovingian period raises potentially disquieting religio-political questions.

There exists in France an organization that has been in continuous existence since the twelfth century, that has some features both of an order of chivalry and of a religious order, though it is not quite either; a secret society which does not spurn the right sort of publicity; a political grouping with specific aims that is also interested in ancient esoteric wisdom and hidden mysteries. Its full name is the Order of the Prieuré Notre-Dame de Sion, and its chief aim seems always to have been the restoration of the Merovingian blood-line to the throne. It is also passionately concerned with the cult of the Black Virgin and has a remarkable record of equal rights for women. One of its female Grand Masters (or Helmsmen), Iolande de Bar (1428-83) lived at Sion-Vaudémont. A detailed account of the Prieuré is to be found in *The Holy Blood and the Holy Grail* by Baigent, Leigh and Lincoln.

Two other authors who have links with the Prieuré, Deloux and Brétigny, suggest that its predilection for the town of Blois as a meeting-place is due in part to the Black Virgin that was venerated there until the Revolution, an exemplar of the one 'who in the era that is drawing to a close is called the Virgin Mary and who remains the eternal Isis'. The authors print a photograph of the Black Virgin of Goult, which they call, in contradistinction to the local guide-book, 'Notre-Dame de Lumière', with the caption 'a Black Virgin particularly venerated by the initiates of the Prieuré of Sion'.

The Grand Master of the Prieuré 1981-4, Pierre Plantard, is reported as saying that the Sicambrians, ancestors of the Frankish Merovingians, worshipped Cybele as Diana of the Nine Fires, or as Arduina, the eponymous goddess of the Ardennes. The huge idol to Diana/Arduina which once towered over Carignan, in north-east France, between the Black Virgin sites of Orval, Avioth and Mezières, near to Stenay, where the Merovingian king and saint, Dagobert II, was murdered in 679, points circumstantially to a link between the two cults. In this connection Plantard mentions that one of the most important acts of Dagobert, when he acceded to the throne after his Irish exile, was to continue the ancient tradition of Gaul, the worship of the Black Virgin. The Black Virgin, he insists, is Isis and her name is Notre-Dame de Lumière.

Why this emphasis on Isis who was, after all, a universal

goddess of countless names? She identifies herself with Artemis of the Cretans and with Cybele when in the *Golden Ass* she tells Apuleius, 'For the Phrygians that are the first of all men call me The Mother of the Gods at Pessinus.' Only the Ethiopians 'of both sort, that dwell in the Orient and are enlightened by the morning rays of the sun, and the Egyptians, which are excellent in all kind of ancient doctrine and by their proper ceremonies accustom to worship me, do call me by my true name, Queen Isis.' But in Gaul, Isis was no more prominent as a universal goddess than Cybele or Artemis/Diana, who have as good a right to be considered precursors of the Black Virgin. May the reason for the Prieuré's insistence on the primacy of Isis not be the importance attached to some Egyptian connection? Victor Belot in *La France des Pélérinages*, referring to Sara, the black Egyptian servant who accompanied her mistresses to Les Saintes Maries de la Mer, writes: 'Sara will give birth to the cult of Black Virgins particularly venerated in certain places, although many authors prefer to leave this privilege to Isis, the Egyptian goddess.' These two possibilities are not, of course, mutually exclusive. In other words, Sara, beloved of the Gypsies, may also be an avatar of Egyptian Isis.

The most important of the three Marys to disembark at what was then still the Isle of Ratis, on whose acropolis Artemis, Isis and Cybele had been worshipped since the fourth century BC, was St Mary Magdalene, whose cult is intertwined with that of another repentant harlot, St Mary the Egyptian. Now, at Orléans, where there is an ancient cult of the Magdalen, St Mary the Egyptian was one of the titles of the Black Virgin. If there is some mystery linking Isis, Egypt, Mary the Egyptian, Mary Magdelene and the Black Virgin, in what way does it involve the Prieuré? Kings often claim illustrious ancestry: the Mikado is the son of Heaven; the British royal line is descended from the gods of the north and the heroes of Troy; the founder of the Ethiopian Empire was the son of the Queen of Sheba and Solomon. What more likely than that the French monarchy should outbid its rivals with an even more dazzling progenitor? According to Lacordaire, who re-established the Dominican Order in France after the Revolution, Louis XI, the most enthusiastic votary the Black Virgin cult has ever known, with attested visits, often repeated, to more than a score of her shrines, regarded Mary

Magdalene as one of the royal line of France. The pious author does not elaborate on this theme, but the secret tradition unearthed by the authors of *The Holy Blood and the Holy Grail* is that the Magdalen brought with her to Les Saintes Maries de la Mer, like a new Queen of Sheba, the fruit of her womb and of the loins of the King of Kings, Jesus Christ. Somehow, this new shoot from the Rod of Jesse became the founder of the Merovingians, though that honour is usually accorded to Mérovée (*c*.374-*c*.425), who was the son both of King Clodio and of a fabulous aquatic beast from beyond the seas. Such is the Holy Blood, and also the Holy Grail (*sang real*) which qualified the Bouillon-Boulogne family to accede by right to the throne of Jerusalem after the first Crusade.

THE SURVIVAL OF THE GODDESS

This is heady stuff, but even if one accepts it literally, as the Prieuré and other contemporaries evidently do, it is difficult to know what to do with the information. It may be that Nostradamus will be proved right and that we shall have to await the outcome of the next war for a new ruler of the ancient root to reveal himself and lead the way to a new order in Europe. But meantime the story is rich in symbolic significance for the travails of our age. Let us look at the history of religion for a moment through the symbols of astrology. At the beginning of the previous epoch, called the Age of Aries, the Ram succeeded the Bull as the sacrificial and symbolic animal. Abraham discovered a ram caught by its horns in a thicket and sacrificed it in place of his son Isaac. Towards the mid-point of the age, Moses, versed 'in all the wisdom of the Egyptians', led his people out of Egypt, received the new commandments on Mount Sinai, and destroyed the Golden Calf. At the beginning of the age of Pisces, Jesus, as the Lamb of God and only begotten son, reversed the process of Abraham's sacrifice by offering himself consciously in place of the animal holocausts in the Temple. Now, as in the calendar of the Platonic Great Year we approach the Aquarian age, something from the Piscean era of Christ, still unrealized and unrecognized, needs to be acknowledged to inaugurate the new dominant of consciousness that a tired world

awaits. 'Out of Egypt have I called my son' (Matthew 2.15). Like
Abraham and Moses, Jesus, too, sojourned in the land of Egypt
whose name means black. If the evidence adduced by Desmond
Stewart in *The Foreigner* is to be credited, then his sojourn may
have been long indeed, lasting well into young manhood. The
wisdom of the Egyptians that he imbibed in Alexandria would
almost certainly have been that of syncretistic Gnosticism, for
whose adherents it was no mere abstraction, but a personified,
divine, feminine principle, which could be experienced. To the
feminine, earthy, cyclical stability of Taurus there had succeeded
the fiery masculine dynamism of Aries and the aggressive
expansion of the great empires. With, finally, Rome's loss of
impetus, and its infiltration by mystical, other-worldly religions
from across the sea, including Christianity, the Piscean influence
strongly affected all strata of society.

Two things happened to interfere with this process away from
the maleness of Aries towards a more intuitive, feeling, 'yin'
approach. One was Christianity's need to differentiate itself
from the increasingly amorphous, syncretistic mood of Hellen-
ism, and distance itself from rivals that at times seemed all too
similar to it. The other was the historical accident, or inter-
vention of the Holy Spirit, which led to a merger between the
Roman imperium and the Christian ecclesia to form Caesaro-
papism and make of it both state religion and party line.

By the beginning of the Christian era the cult of the Olympian
deities was in decline. Worship of Jupiter, as of Caesar, belonged
to the official religion and had little power to stir the hearts of
those who sought salvation and the assurance of immortality.
The cult of the great goddesses, allied to Olympus for a while,
but antedating it, retained its old prestige and fervour in many
places. The mysteries of Demeter and Persephone at Eleusis
greatly prospered under the Roman Empire, while from Ephesus
to Marseilles the prerogatives of Artemis remained unassailable,
even by St Paul.

Such evidence as exists suggests that, throughout the Celtic
world, worship of the Triple Mother (Deae Matres) and of the
Mare-Goddess, Epona, remained of considerable importance
throughout the Roman ascendancy. Furthermore, the three great
goddesses from the east, Isis, Cybele and Diana of the Ephesians,
all on occasions represented as black, had already established

themselves in the west in pre-Roman times. The Phocaeans, from their base at Marseilles, founded in 600BC, spread the fame of their patroness Artemis, a replica of the Ephesian, far and wide along the Mediterranean littoral from Antibes to Barcelona and beyond, as well as into the Gallic heartland of their allies the Arverni, and wherever their traders forged or followed the tin-routes. This Massiliot sphere of influence happens to correspond to those areas where the greatest concentration of Black Virgins is to be found.

But in the later centuries of the rule of Rome, it was the more exotic cults of Isis and Cybele that aroused the greatest enthusiasm and the largest congregations. The west welcomed the great universal goddess as a phenomenon neither alien nor imposed from without. Lyons, capital of the Three Gauls, was already the city of Cybele by the third century, while in Paris Isis reigned until St Genevieve took over her attributes as the new patroness of the city.

As late as the fourth century it must have seemed probable to a contemporary observer that, if the Empire survived, a religion of consensus would predominate based on the worship of the universal Great Mother and her son/consort, sacrificed for the salvation of many. Protestant critics of Rome were later to aver that, Empire or not, this was precisely what had occurred. But the Christian Church that Constantine established was, for various reasons, undergoing a strongly masculine phase. First, the courage it had displayed under the persecutions of Decius and Diocletian, which had so greatly impressed Constantine, called for the defiant steadfastness and simple faith of Christian soldiers in both its male and female martyrs, rather than subtler, gentler, more ambiguous qualities. It was, furthermore, with just such qualities that the Church, by creeds and definitions, had been at grips for two centuries in the form of Christian Gnosticism, ever elusive and diffuse in its quest for feminine wisdom and subjective, experiential truth.

The Church that emerged had many of the characteristics of a suddenly victorious resistance movement and was, all too humanly, unsympathetic towards former foes, fellow-travellers and those who had shown little stomach for the fight. It also inherited the Roman virtue of sound organization, based on a powerful central authority, and preserved by strict legalism. One consequence of Caesaro-papism was that failure to toe the party line became a new crime, called heresy, which was vigorously suppressed wherever possible. In the far corners of the Empire, however, such as Edessa, the headquarters of Syrian Christianity, home of the first Christian Church and the first icon, freer reign was given to the imagination. From that area stemmed the earliest version of the Assumption of Mary, and the first liturgy and hymns in her honour.

The Marian stream flowing from Edessa became a torrent when, at Ephesus in AD431, in the interests of deterring heresy as well as of honouring the Virgin, she was declared Theotokos, the Mother of God. This occurred in the home town of the first and greatest temple of Artemis, as well as of Mary herself in her last years.

Thus, in the Empire of the East, the hyperdulia accorded to Mary, a step short of the worship of God but superior to the veneration that is offered to the saints, perpetuated the preceding cult of Wisdom and the Great Mother. In AD438 the Empress Eudoxia sent to her sister-in-law the Empress Pulcheria an icon of the Virgin painted by St Luke, which, with the possible exception of a second-century mural from the catacomb of Priscilla in Rome, is the first recorded image of Our Lady. Pulcheria became an enthusiastic collector of relics pertaining to the Virgin and helped to set the fashion for holy images which flourished wherever Byzantium held sway, until the iconoclastic controversy of the seventh and eighth centuries caused a temporary set-back.

HISTORICAL SURVEY OF THE BLACK VIRGIN CULT IN THE WEST

Eudoxia's image became known as the Nicopoeion, Creator of Victory, and, indeed, under the sign of Mary, 'terrible as an army with banners', the old Empire of the East was to maintain its integrity against foes within and without for a further thousand years. In the west, however, a very different situation prevailed. In 410 Rome was sacked, and, within half a century, the Visigoths ruled from the Loire to Andalucia, with Franks to the north, Burgundians to the east and Vandals to the south.

Neither the Celts nor the Teutonic invaders had a strong ancient tradition of anthropomorphic deities worshipped in temples built with hands. Once the Roman influence had been withdrawn, it seems probable that most rural areas were content to revert to simpler ways, whether Christian or pagan. The well-organized Christian groups under their bishops, many of them powerful personalities, became the representatives of their communities, replacing the imperial bureaucracy as a possible body with whom the new rulers could treat. Monasticism, which started in the east, was, by the time of the invasions, well-established in Gaul thanks to such pioneering founders as St Martin (AD 360), St Honoratus (410) and John Cassian (406/415). It helped to preserve learning and civilization, provided a training-school for effective leaders and, as in the case of Cassian's twin foundation for men and women in Marseilles, underlined the role of women in the Church and provided a focus for the cult of the Virgin. At some point during the fifth century the temple of Isis at Soissons was rededicated to the Blessed Virgin, and, in 410, Cybele processed in her ox-cart for the last time through the streets of Autun. Le Puy was already consecrated to Mary by AD 225, though her first apparition there (AD 46/7) rivals that of Zaragoza (AD 40). The irruption of the Christian, though heretically Arian, Visigoths into Gaul accelerated the decline of paganism in the lands they controlled and the transition to the Christian Goddess.

It is to the Merovingian period (AD 500-750) that many of the Black Virgin shrines of France trace their origins. Our Lady of Boulogne sailed into the harbour standing in a boat with no sails or crew, but containing a copy of the Gospels in Syriac, while King Dagobert I was attending Sunday Mass. The legendary date for the consecration of the crypt is AD 46 but, in its present form, it was built by St Ida, mother of Godefroy de Bouillon, conqueror of Jerusalem and founder of the Prieuré, whose tomb is there. The Black Virgin Cult of Mauriac dates from 507, when Theodechilde, daughter of Clovis, first Christian king of the Franks, found, haloed by light in a forest clearing, a statuette guarded by a lioness and her cubs. Clovis met his queen, Clotilde, at Ferrières, the first Christian village in Gaul, where the cult of the Black Virgin had its legendary origin in AD 44. Not long after the destruction of church and town by Attila (AD

461), the Merovingian dynasty lavishly restored and augmented the cult, and its last reigning members made it their place of residence.

The ninth century was an important era for the cult of the Black Virgin. In 888, not long after the liberation of Barcelona, the little, dark Madonna of Montserrat was discovered by shepherds in the mountain cave where, long before, a Gothic bishop had hidden her from the Moors. At roughly the same period another Virgin, destined to become the patroness of her people, Our Lady of the Dark Forest, was carried up by St Meinrad to the Hermitage where the Abbey of Einsiedeln now stands. A monk of Mont St Michel, where Louis XI was to found his order of chivalry, visited the Holy Land in 867, where he would have been in a position to acquire sacred images, though it is possible that devotion to the statue of Our Lady of the Dead at Mont-Tombe in the crypt of the abbey church dates from even earlier. In 876 Charles the Bald transferred the chemise (*chainze*) of the Virgin from Aachen to Chartres, where the cult of a holy well 'of the strong', and of 'The Virgin Who Will Give Birth', Our Subterranean Lady, has been attributed to the Druidic era.

But the age, *par excellence*, of Our Lady, when she began to be venerated by that name, was inaugurated when the Crusaders, with a new marching song from Le Puy, the 'Salve Regina', on their lips, embarked on the mission entrusted to them at Clermont, of winning Jerusalem back for Christendom. To the battle cry of 'God wills it!', Godefroy de Bouillon's army stormed Jerusalem in 1099 and on his death shortly afterwards, his brother Baldwin was proclaimed first Latin king of the world capital of the three great religions known to the west. Some eighteen years later a small party of knights appeared, ostensibly charged with the task of patrolling the Jaffa-Jerusalem road and protecting pilgrims, though it seems doubtful that a mere nine cavalrymen, mounted, according to tradition, two to a horse to emphasise their poverty, would have proved an effective police force for this purpose. In fact, however, their mission seems to have been more enigmatic, since they were housed in a wing of the royal palace on the site of Solomon's Temple. This setting, which appears needlessly lavish for knights vowed to a life of penury, as well as unsound tactically as a highway patrol barracks, earned them their name, the Order of the Temple. The

2. Guadalupe

Temple, it has been speculated, was indeed what they had come to investigate, and the object of their quest nothing less than the Ark of the Covenant, the very presence of God that tabernacled with the Children of Israel during the years of Exodus from Egypt, placed by Solomon in the Holy of Holies at the heart of the Temple he built for it, and which, perchance, still lay hidden in the foundations after the ravages of Nebuchadnezzar and the Romans. Unless, as the Ethiopian tradition maintains, Solomon had already bestowed it on the son he shared with the Queen of Sheba. I once asked a member of one of the Orders which succeeded the Templars at their dissolution what was the symbolic meaning of the Black Virgin. He answered by another question: 'What did the Templars go to look for in Jerusalem?'

Another quest object and sacred container, unheard of before the twelfth century, but universally famous by the time of the massacre of Montségur, was the Holy Grail. In its first literary manifestation, the author, Chrétien de Troyes, makes a bizarre connection, generally attributed to ignorance or inadvertency, when, into this Celtic fable, he introduces the wife of Solomon. Wolfram von Eschenbach, in his slightly later version *Parzival* claimed as his source Kyot de Provins, a troubadour and apologist for the Templars. Curiously enough, the last earthly guardian of the Grail was Parzival's nephew, Prester John, a mysterious Priest-King, like Melchizedek of Jerusalem, whose realm included India and Ethiopia. He is yet another phenomenon of questionable tangibility to emerge from the twelfth century. He had, however, by 1177, achieved sufficient prestige and reality for Pope Alexander III to address him in a letter as 'King of the Indies, most holy priest'. Prester John had previously written (1165) to his friends, 'The Emperor of Rome and the King of France'; describing himself as 'by the grace of God, King over all Christian kings'. He tells of his capital, which has many of the features of a Grail castle, and of the strange fauna and flora of his country, including a pair of Alerions, the heraldic birds of the House of Lorraine which Godefroy of Bouillon substituted for the Merovingian bees on his escutcheon.

Of the two chief candidates in the west to be considered the Castle of the Grail, one is Montségur, site in 1244 of the last stand of the Cathars, those heretical champions of the religion of Amor against Roma and of the civilization of Oc against the barbarism of the north. The other is Montserrat, home of La Moreneta, where Wagner was inspired to compose his *Parsifal* and St Ignatius hung up his sword. Glastonbury, where, according to legend, St Joseph of Arimathea built in AD 63 the first church in Britain and dedicated it to the Virgin, has long been associated with the Holy Grail. Joseph arrived on these shores with 150 followers on a miraculous shirt (*chainze?*), while the remainder of his retinue, who had been unable to keep their vows of abstinence during the journey, crossed the Channel more prosaically on a ship built by King Solomon. A possible predecessor of St Joseph's as a proto-missionary was Aristobulus, a name famous in early Alexandrian syncretism, but better known to us as Zebedee, the husband of Mary Salome and the father of St James of Compostela, who, presumably after the voyage with them to Les Saintes Maries de la Mer, though his name does not feature on the passenger list, continued northward to bear the good news to this island.

ST BERNARD AND THE RELIGION OF OUR LADY

These were potent legends in their day, and if viewed as part of the history of ideas that have stirred the imagination of our ancestors and influenced their attitudes, rather than as concrete historical facts, they merit sympathetic understanding. A passionate longing is at the heart of the matter — something is lost that by the twelfth century desperately needs to be found. If it is the Holy Grail, then it is to Christians a secret about Christ's new commandment of love, expressed in His passion, crucifixion and resurrection, and his nourishing presence with those of pure heart who ask the right question. But, as a symbol, it is also at one with the magic cauldrons of Cerridwen and the Dagda in Celtic lore, with Medea's vessel of transformation and the pot in which Odin spirited away the mead that inspires poetry and wisdom.

If it is the Ark of the Covenant we seek, we must first turn to Moses, trained in the Egyptian mysteries, who kept within it the tables of the law, summation of the new dispensation, and some of the daily, supersubstantial bread of heaven that fed the Israelites in the wilderness. It also housed Aaron's magic wand, which, like the Rod of Jesse and Joseph of Arimathea's staff, contains within itself an ardent shoot (Plant-ard?), a spirit of spontaneous regeneration potential to matter, that has the power to burgeon at unexpected times and places. But we must look back, too, to the Ark of Noah in which life was preserved on Earth during the Flood, and, since in twelfth-century Latin the words are one, up to the arch in the heavens, which was the solution to the Flood, as well as forward to the pointed arch that was the wonder of that surprisingly named phenomenon, Gothic art. In or off the great nave-vessels of the Gothic churches and cathedrals, or in the crypts below, we find the statues of Our Lady in whose name all this beauty was created. It is especially when she appears in her black form, as a Virgin of the Crusades, that we should meditate on the title given her in the Litany of Loreto, *Arca foederis*, Ark of the Covenant, a motif underlined in the symbolism of Chartres Cathedral. Finally we might do well to cast a sideways glance, since riddlers and puzzlers delight in the subtle word-play, sometimes called green language, or the language of birds, at Arcas, the bear, doubly constellated in the heavens, attribute of Artemis, Arthur and Dagobert II, a fabulous beast, evocative of Arcadia and its sacred mysteries.

Amid all the legends and riddles of the twelfth century one historical character stands out as incomparably the most important figure of his day, who provides a golden thread through most of the themes of which we have been treating, St Bernard of Clairvaux. Born at Fontaines, said to have possessed its own Black Virgin, on the outskirts of Dijon, where the ancient Lady of Good Hope already reigned, he received while still a boy three drops of milk from the breast of the Black Virgin of Châtillon. Inspired by this, he took the ailing new Order of Cîteaux, reduced to a handful of monks, and turned it into a vast multinational enterprise of civilization, spanning Europe and making it prosper through hundreds of Abbeys from Russia to the furthest west, each one dedicated to Our Lady. In 1128 he wrote the rule of the Order of the Temple. Among the Templars' founder members were Bernard's uncle, André de Montbard and Hugues de Payen, first Grand Master of the Temple and of the Prieuré. The Templars, imprisoned and awaiting death in the Castle of Chinon after the coup of 1307, composed a prayer to Our Lady acknowledging Bernard to be the founder of her religion. In addition to the numerous hymns and sermons he addressed to her, he wrote about 280 sermons on the theme of the Song of Songs, the epithalamion of Solomon and the Queen of Sheba, whose versicle 'I am black, but I am beautiful, O ye daughters of Jerusalem', is the recurring refrain of the Black Virgin cult. Marina Warner hints that Bernard's visit to Rome inspired the mosaic in St Maria de Trastevere, the first in Rome for three centuries, in which the Virgin is shown as the beloved Shulamite from the 'Song of Songs', bride of Solomon and Christ. He encouraged the pilgrimage to Compostela, sometimes called the Milky Way, star-studded with Templar commanderies, Benedictine or Cistercian hostelries and churches of the Black Virgin. From one of the four great starting-points, Vézelay, centre of the cult of the Magdalen and subsequent Black Virgin site, he preached the Second Crusade. After his death, this holy lover of Our Lady acquired, on his canonization, the same feast day, 20 August, as St Amadour, founder of Rocamadour. Canonization makes some strangely appropriate bedfellows, as we shall see later, especially in Chapter 4.

St Bernard was familiar with the Cathars and their doctrines, having carried out an arduous and unsuccessful preaching campaign in their midst. He also had much respect for and interest in Islamic lore in spite of launching the Second Crusade. St Malachy, the last of the great Irish holy men of the Middle Ages to make their mark on Europe, to whom were attributed the celebrated prophecies concerning all future popes, was his close friend and died in his arms. Although it is not explicit in his writings, it is plausible to deduce from his actions that Bernard cherished the vision of a new world order based on the three pillars of the Benedictines, the Cistercians and the Templars, under a King of Kings. Thus the theocratic ideal of Godefroy de Bouillon would have found fulfilment.

But in this monk, extraversion was always balanced by spiritual inwardness, and the divine harmony, potential within each individual, interested him no less than the affairs of Church and State. In this age of the troubadours and the courts of love Bernard could be seen as the first troubadour of Our Lady, whose favours he had received and whose image he carried in his heart. In this he was reverting to the tradition of a major source of troubadour poetry, Sufism, in which the beloved is symbolic and spiritual. In the west, La Dame, although physically real, was also the inspiring glorious presence, leading the lover along the path and protecting him in danger. She is Goethe's 'eternal feminine' and the muse of all true poets. Denis de Rougemont, the author of *Passion and Society*, surmises that La Dame is the anima, the spiritual part of man, the archetypal content which, according to Jung, may be the messenger of the Grail, linking a man to the inner journey of the individuation process. John Layard attests that Bernard, who at times seems almost possessed by the positive anima, had also a remarkable psychological understanding of her negative repressed aspect when he describes 'Eve within the soul', as 'that lady who lies at home paralysed and grievously tormented'.

Neither the cult of the Black Virgin nor the art of the troubadours died with the twelfth century, but the new flowering of the feminine principle to which it had given birth suffered a deadly blow. Rome allied itself with the King of France and the mercenary barons of the north to unleash against the heartland of southern civilization the Albigensian Crusade. Much more than Catharism withered in the ensuing blight: the courts of the inquisition replaced the courts of love; so-called heretics, men and women, were tortured and massacred; and, when the inquisitors' original victims were no more, they turned their attention to so-called witchcraft to fuel their fires for another half millennium. The mantle of courtesy passed from Languedoc to Italy as the terrible fourteenth century brought the slander and destruction of the Templars, the Hundred Years War and the Black Death.

The witch pyres of Europe were extinguished late in time by the cold douche of the Age of Reason. Less cruel and murderous than the age of superstition, it was hardly less inimical to all that is meant by the feminine principle. The revolutionary devotees of what they called the Goddess Reason were at one with their high-minded Protestant predecessors in seeing the little Black Virgins as an archetypal opposite to all they stood for, a symbol older and more formidable than King or Pope, of that elemental and uncontrollable source of life, possessing a spirit and wisdom of its own not subject to organization or the laws of rationality. In the nineteenth century, popular enthusiasm broke through the encrusting intellectual superiority of the clerisy in the direct experience of Our Lady manifest at Lourdes, La Salette, rue du Bac and Knock. This wave of devotion reanimated the ancient devotion to the Black Virgins, many of which were solemnly crowned by authority of the Pope during the period 1860-90. The twentieth century has witnessed further apparitions, some, like those of Fatima, Banneux and Beauraing, authorized as genuine cults by the Church, others, like Garabandal and Zeitoun, blossoming as unofficial roses.

Synchronous with these archetypal phenomena, whether they are viewed as hysterical mass hallucinations or as psychic realities, the most striking and influential sociological development of the past century in the west has been the sexual revolution — the emancipation of women through education, equal rights, divorce, birth-control, legal abortion and greater freedom of sexual choice. Such liberty, not unknown to the Celtic women of old, was repressed during the Christian era, and has had to struggle to re-emerge in the teeth of opposition by the Church.

The return of the Black Virgin to the forefront of collective consciousness has coincided with the profound psychological need to reconcile sexuality and religion. She has always helped her supplicants to circumvent the rigidities of patriarchal legislation and is traditionally on the side of physical processes — healing the sick, easing the pangs of childbirth, making the milk flow. She knows how to break rigid masculine rules, bringing dead babies back to life long enough to receive baptism and escape from limbo to paradise, looking with tolerance on the sins of the flesh as when she acts as midwife to a pregnant abbess or stands in for a truant nun tasting for a time the illicit pleasures of sin. Politically, she is in favour of freedom and integrity, the right of peoples, cities and nations to be inviolate and independent from outside interference. Nowhere is this more evident than in the history of the Queen of Poland, the Black Madonna of Czestochowa.

CHAPTER 1
The influence of the east

There can be no sure historical beginning to our story. The wheel, whether it be spun by Hindu Maya, Roman Fortuna, British Arianrhod or Christian Catherine of Alexandria, revolves in endless cycles between Yin and Yang. In spinning a tale, however, one must start somewhere, with a 'once upon a time', with a something that happened 'in illo tempore'. Once upon a time men, carried away by technological hubris and over-weening aggression against the heavens, constructed Babel. Excessive Yang provoked the Yin of the great waters and the one-sidedness was swept clean. Life re-emerged with a raven and a dove from the ark of the coupling, a rainbow linked the opposites, and the first wine was made. Once upon a time there were small townships that depended on horticulture. They were replaced by cities dependent on intensive farming to feed them and on great armies to defend them. Once upon a time Gilgamesh and Enkidu cut down the tree of the great goddess, and restless peoples from the north and east, Aryan followers of the headstrong ram, slew the bull of heaven and subjugated its mistress to their male deities, although never wholly.

Yet, if there is no beginning, there is at least a text — and a biblical one — which catches the spirit and essence of our story: 'I am black but beautiful' (Song of Solomon 1.5). Who is the beloved who sings this refrain to her lover? All we are told of her is that she is a Shulamite, that is, one who has found peace, perhaps the counterpart of Solomon whose name also contains the word 'shalom'. Jerusalem is the city of peace where Solomon built his Temple for the Shekinah, the feminine, indwelling, glorious presence of God, and Jerusalem will be the bride of Christ at the consummation of the aeons. Undoubtedly the black beauty is the Lady Anima, who has stimulated the fantasies and aroused the projections of men throughout the centuries. The stern moralists and champions of scholarly orthodoxy, Bernard and Aquinas, who both cast out nature with a pitch-fork in youth, devoted their most fervent later meditations to the love story of the dark lady. Sometimes she is Pharaoh's daughter, the wisdom of the Egyptians, but more often she is seen as Solomon's most famous lover, the Queen of Sheba, who came to try him with hard questions. Sheba can mean 'seven', i.e. the planets, or 'oath', a solemn vow or covenant witnessed and enforced by the heavenly powers. It is also the realm of the Sabeans, a people early synonymous with astrologers and later with Gnostics, whom Islam tolerated, along with Jews and Christians, as one of the peoples of the book. Jesus refers to her favourably (Matthew 12.42) as the Queen of the South who will rise up to condemn unbelievers at the Last Judgment. The Queen of the South is also the title of the Countess of Toulouse, city whose Black Virgin, La Daurade, was originally the goddess of wisdom, Pallas Athene. Meridiana, a noon-day enchantress from the warm south, seduced Gerbert of Aurillac (qv) and gave him such wisdom that he became the most learned man of his age, Pope of the year 1000, the first Frenchman to sit on the throne of Peter.

Differing accounts exist of the Queen of Sheba's true country. In one version the hoopoe, who taught Solomon the language of birds, described a wonderful land of which he knew nothing, the only part of the world not under his control. In the Qu'ran (Sura 27) Solomon learns that a woman reigns over this people, possessed of every virtue and of a splendid throne, but who worship the sun rather than Allah. He invites this Queen to visit him and she arrives at Sion accompanied by a camel-train laden with unparalleled riches in gold, spices and precious stones. Solomon is, however, suspicious of his guest's credentials: if she is a djinn she will have hairy legs like a wild-ass or a wild-goat. He therefore arranges for her to approach him in a room with a glass floor so that he can see under her skirts. In another version, he sits on the far side of a stream to see if she will use the bridge made of the wood of the true Cross. The Queen recognizes it, not surprisingly, since, in an earlier incarnation, it had been the tree of paradise and she the serpent, so she wades instead across the water, hoisting her skirts to reveal what Solomon wanted to see, her hairy legs. Neither of them seems much put out and Solomon restores the limbs to pristine comeliness by means of a special depilatory he has prepared. It would seem then that Solomon did not find her and the particular religious tradition she represented altogether unacceptable, a tolerance which accords with his reputation of introducing foreign ways into Israel.

In the Kebra Nagast, the Ethiopian 'Book of the Glory of the Kings' (c.13th century), the founder of the Ethiopian dynasty is named as Menelek ('son of the wise'), offspring of Solomon and the Queen of Sheba. (This tradition is enshrined in the Ethiopian constitution of 1955 which states that Haile Selassie was a direct descendant of Menelek.) The Queen's name here is Makeda, 'the fiery one', which might link her to that fiery, hirsute, wandering star, the comet (= 'hairy' in Greek). It was such a star that led the Magi, like the sons of Noah returning to the Ark, along with 'all from Saba' (Mass for Epiphany), to Mary, the new Ark of the Covenant who first displayed the precious content of her womb to the world in Bethlehem at Epiphany. In the Middle Ages the Magi were known as the Three Kings of Cologne, city of Roman, Celt and Teuton, where two Black Virgins reign. Since 1355 one of the Kings has been traditionally represented as Black. According to Michel Tournier the Black King is Caspar, the monarch of Sudanese Meroë (Mérovée?) the bearer of gold whose name means 'the white one'. More often the black Magus is considered to be Melchior, 'king of light', whose gift is myrrh, signifying entombment. Epiphany is also the feast of St Melanius, 'the black', a fifth-century Celt from Brittany, and the only saint of this name in the calendar.

The Queen of Sheba, in a legend from the borders of Ethiopia and Eritrea, was a Tigre girl known as Eteye Azeb ('queen of the south') who was tied half-way up a tree as an offering to a dragon. Seven saints, resting under the tree, alerted to her presence by tears falling on them, rescued her and slew the dragon by means of the Cross. She returned to her village where she was elected chief and chose another young woman as her deputy. But some dragon's blood had splashed her heel transforming it into that of an ass. She set off with her lieutenant to be healed by King Solomon, after which the story follows much the same course as the other versions except that she gives birth to Menelek, on whom his father, Solomon, bestows the Ark of the Covenant. In one variation of the saga from the

Christian west, Queen Sibylla, as she is called, the ancestress of all magicians, has the webbed foot of a water-fowl rather than a hoof. In this she resembles La Reine Pédauque, identified with Charlemagne's mother, the Merovingian princess, Bertha of the Big Foot. She conceived him between Liesse, home of the favourite Black Virgin of the French monarchs, and Laon (qv), where there is a Black Virgin and a statue of the Eritrean sybil who prophesies the end of the world. There, too, a phial of the Virgin's milk was venerated until 1789. Pépin le Bref later married Bertha in order to legitimize his usurpation of the throne. Other authorities have traced La Reine Pédauque's origins to Austris, 'south wind', wife of Euric, the Visigothic ruler of Toulouse, in whose church of the Black Virgin, La Daurade, she was buried. She is associated with a bridge, a subterranean aqueduct and a magic distaff, one of the symbols of Athene.

The distaff, sign of practical feminine wisdom, is woman's magic wand of transformation in that almost alchemical process, the production of linen from flax. The third of the riddles posed by the Queen of Sheba to Solomon had as its answer the word 'flax'. The mid-day demoness of the Wends, Pripolniza, appeared in the fields between midday and two o'clock to subject any people still foolish enough to be abroad to a searching examination on the cultivation of flax and the weaving of linen, punishing those who failed by cutting off their heads and carrying them away with her. Similar tales are told of the Pshesponiza of the Spreewald, near Berlin, and the Serpolnica of the Serbs. Freyja, too, from her name Horn, is a flax-goddess. Quite possibly two of the suggested prototypes of La Reine Pédauque, Bertha of the Big Foot and Bertha of Burgundy, tenth-century Queen of France, have become confused with the Teutonic mother-goddess, one of whose attributes was the distaff. De Sède suggests that the confusion between Bertha and the Reine Pédauque may stem from the punning association of Bertha and 'bertel', the word for a distaff in the language of Oc. The pun-language of birds familiar to Solomon through the hoopoe, who was the Queen of Sheba's father, was rediscovered by the troubadors of Toulouse. They would have appreciated the similarity between La Reine Pédauque, the queen with the goosefoot, and La Reine du Pays d'Oc. They would also have noted Reine de Saba, *reino sabo* (wise queen).

This queen of many disguises has had an extensive mythology within the Christian epoch. It may just be an amusing coincidence that the spirit of Epiphany in Germany is known as Frau Bertha, who has very large feet and an iron nose, a nursery demoness who lulls good children to sleep, but is the terror of the badly behaved. In England, the morrow of the Epiphany used to be known as St Distaff's Day or Rock Day, after an old name for the distaff. Marie-Louise von Franz identifies her with Maria the Jewess or Prophetess, the greatest woman alchemist. Honorius of Autun (early twelfth century) in his commentary on the Song of Solomon sees the Queen of the South as a figure of the Church which is the queen and concubine of Christ. To complete the equation, St Gregory the Great (540-604) relates the south and its wind to the unseen orders of angels and the heat of the Holy Spirit. A link is thus forged between the Queen of the South, the Queen of Sheba, the black Shulamite of the Song of Solomon and Maria the Alchemist. In a later chapter the connection between this underground stream of the repressed goddess and the cult of Mary Magdelene, whom the Gnostics saw as the lover of Christ, and the Black Virgin will be fully considered. In the camarín of the Black Virgin of Guadalupe, the Statue of Miriam, Moses' sister, is called Maria Prophetissa.

In her various forms, the figure we are discussing has always been a favourite of writers. Anatole France's alchemical novel is called *La Rôtisserie de la Reine Pédauque*. In Flaubert's *Temptation of St Antony* the Queen of Sheba represents luxuria, the deadly sin of lust (Venus, goddess of love, rides a goose and is drawn in a swan-chariot). A comparable image is to be found in the writings of Gérard de Nerval (1808-55), the troubadour of the anima and of the disconsolate Prince of Aquitaine whose tower has been destroyed. His fatal obsession with Aurélia gives a remarkable impression of the quality of this figure. He tells of 'the Queen of the South, such as I saw her in my dreams ... crowned with stars, in a turban sparkling with the colours of the rainbow ... her face is olive-tinted ... one foot is on a bridge, the other on a wheel ... one hand rests on the highest rock of the mountains in the Yemen, the other stretched out to the heavens holds . . . the flower of fire . . . the celestial serpent opens its maw to seize it . . . the Sign of the Ram appears twice in the zodiac, which reflects the face of the Queen as in a mirror, a face which takes on the features of St Rosalie . . . she appears, crowned with stars, ready to save the world . . . on the peak of the highest mountain of the Yemen a wonderful bird is singing in a cage . . . it is the talisman of the new ages . . . Leviathan with black wings flies heavily around . . . beyond the sea there rises another peak on which is written this name: Mérovée.' Nerval hanged himself from a lamp-post at dawn on 26 January 1855, with the manuscript of *Aurélia*, it is said, in his pocket. In 1862 Gounod produced an opera *The Queen of Sheba* based on this story.

Christianity reached Ethiopia in apostolic times when Philip the Deacon converted and baptised the eunuch-treasurer of Queen Candace (Acts 7.26-39). Candace seems to have been the title of the Queens of Ethiopia in Hellenistic times, as well as the name of a Queen of Tarsus who seduced Alexander the Great into a life of sloth, or accidie. This is one of the afflictions meted out by Meridiana, the noonday demoness. Candace is another manifestation of the Queen of Sheba archetype. As Nerval knew, her true country, in so far as it has a local habitation and a name, is neither Ethiopia nor Egypt but the Yemen, the Saba where flax was grown and gold abounded. Near the ancient capital of Marib stood the great shrine of Mahram Bilquis, one of the most strongly fortified sites of southern Arabia, probably designed by Phoenician architects between the eleventh and ninth centuries BC, when they also were building the Temple of Jerusalem. This seems to have been the Temple of the moon god Ilmuqah who, though masculine, is the same as the goddess Ishtar, and the Queen of Sheba, locally known as Bilqis/Balqis. Charles Nodier, Grand Master of the Prieuré de Sion and mentor of de Nerval, wrote of her as Belkiss in *La Fée aux Miettes*. His disciple, closest friend and successor as Nautonier of the Prieuré, Victor Hugo, called her by the name under which she is now presenting herself to the world, Lilith.

LILITH

Considering her successful literary career, Lilith remains surprisingly little known to the educated public. Alfred de Vigny, another friend of Nodier's, writes of her as the spirit of night, Adam's mistress, the rival and enemy of Eve and her children. Victor Hugo makes of her Satan's eldest daughter, the black soul of the world, the great woman of the shadow, the savage and eternal blackness of night, who is fate and Isis. Lilith and Isis have in common their knowledge of the secret name of God. Anatole France, the ironist and admirer of Black Virgins, who wrote a two-volume life of Joan of Arc, included among his novels *Thaïs*, the story of the repentant whore of Egypt who became a saint, and, in 1889, *La Fille de Lilith*. D. G. Rossetti tells of her vengeance on Adam and Eve, and Goethe finds a place for her in his description of Walpurgisnacht. She appears in Shaw's *Back to Methuselah* and as Sabine/Lily in *The Skin of Our Teeth* by Thornton Wilder, played seductively on the London stage by Vivien Leigh. Berg's opera *Lulu* and Wedekind's *Pandora's Box*, on which it is largely based, are both inspired by the myth of Lilith and her repression. George MacDonald's *Lilith* presents a faithful portrait of the archetype. Anaïs Nin consecrated one of her erotic tales in *Delta of Venus* to a character called Lilith. In films, Lilith has been played by Jean Seberg and Marianne Faithfull (in *Lucifer Rising*).

Who then is this figure who has come to stand for feminine rebellion against masculine denial of woman's right to freedom and equality? The earliest known portrait of her, dating from c.1950 BC, is the terra-cotta Burney relief in the British Museum. In it she is depicted as a beautiful, winged, naked woman with the feet of a bird (a cock, thought the cabbalists), standing on two lions and flanked by a pair of owls, with an ephah, for measuring grain, in her hand. Her turban is somewhat reminiscent of that of the Black Virgin of Meymac and her hands are raised hieratically to shoulder height.

As 'the hand of Inanna', the task of the young maiden Lilith in Erech was to gather men from the streets and bring them to the temple of the goddess. But she is best known as one of the Sumerian demons of storm and night. Her main function seems to have been that of a vampirish succuba. Originally her nest was in the middle of the Huluppu tree — probably a willow — a position later much favoured by Black Virgins. Like Wotan's Yggdrasil, Lilith's tree had a dragon at its base and a bird

3. Meymac

perching on top. The hero Gilgamesh, though his own father may have been a Lillu-demon, killed the dragon and cut down the tree, obliging the now homeless Lilith to flee into the wilderness. A seventh-century tablet from Syria shows her as a winged sphinx, a creature notorious for its riddles but in this case evidently more to be feared as a killer of new-born infants. It was above all in this role that she was most redoubted by the Jews from the eighth century BC, though she was also well-known as a seductive — and destructive — nocturnal temptress. Her main threat to Orthodox Judaism may have been the recurrent temptation to the cult of the goddess.

The explanation for such behaviour had to await an eleventh-century cabbalistic document, 'The Alphabet of Ben Sira'. According to this tradition, the first man and woman were created simultaneously from the same substance, with equal rights as the primal androgynous being, joined together at the rear. A conflict arose as to the best position to adopt during sexual intercourse. Lilith resented Adam's pretensions to superiority and her consequent relegation to a passive, supine role. In her despair she invoked the ineffable name of Yahweh, and was forthwith granted wings with which she flew from the paradise that had become her prison. Three angels were sent to recapture her, but she remained obdurate. She was sentenced to give birth to innumerable progeny, of which one hundred would perish daily. Crushed at the cruelty of the punishment, she cast herself into the Red Sea, at which the angels, pitying her sorrow, accorded her power over all new-born babies, for eight days in the case of boys and for twenty in the case of girls, while children born out of wedlock would be permanently at her mercy. Any infant protected by an amulet bearing the names of the angels would be immune from her attentions. Powers of life and death over new-born babies are attributed to many Black Virgins.

After the death of Abel, Adam abstained from Eve for 130 years, during which time he received the secret visits of Lilith. One of their offspring conceived during this period was a wise frog who taught the languages of men, animals and birds as well as the healing properties of herbs and precious stones. By the middle of the thirteenth century, when the cult of the Black Virgin was well-established, the vindication of Lilith reached the point where a Spanish cabbalist described her as 'a ladder on which one can ascend to the rungs of prophecy'. In the sixteenth-century cabbala she is seen covered with hair from head to foot, like Mary Magdalene, Mary the Egyptian and other repentant harlots, leading her band of demonesses in wild, sardana-like round-dances.

Repressed gods take their captors captive. Both Lilith and, as we shall see, Wotan, insinuate themselves into the cults that succeed them. Thus Lilith, from being an abhorred demoness, becomes the bride of Yahweh, the spirit of the diaspora, after the destruction of the Temple. In a notable case of divine wife-swapping, Lilith, wife of Samael/Satan, changes places with the Matronit, consort of Yahweh. In the contrast between Lilith and Matronit we might perhaps see a parallel with the opposing pairs, Mary, Queen of Heaven, and Mary Magdalene; White Virgin and Black Virgin; Church and Synagogue; orthodoxy and heresy. As goddess of the underground religious stream, Lilith fostered the development of the cabbala in Saracen Spain: the cabbala flourished mightily during Israel's sojourn there and fecundated the nascent mysticism of the Christian — and not so Christian — west.

Lilith has no mention in the Authorized Version of the Bible. In Isaiah 34.14 she appears as a screech-owl, a name still given to the witches of Italy and Switzerland, which is amended in the Revised Standard Version as 'night-hag', though the Septuagint, more familiar with such creatures, calls her 'Lamia'. The French Jerusalem Bible, in addition to the Isaiah references, has Lilith (Job 18.15) dwelling in the tent of the wicked. She appears also in the Bible in a number of other forms under other names. Of her identity with the Queen of Sheba in the cabbala, the Zohar and Arabic legends, there is no doubt. She is also associated with the concubine of Abraham, Hagar 'the Egyptian', whose son, Ishmael, having been begotten on the Black Stone of the Ka'aba, became the ancestor of the Arab peoples. It was Lilith and her companion, Naamah, who elicited the famous judgment of Solomon over the child whose ownership they disputed. One of her incarnations was no doubt Moses' first desert wife, Zipporah ('female bird'), and perhaps even his second, called 'the Ethiopian woman', whose dusky beauty distinguished her from other women. When asked by her father Jethro who had rescued her (Exodus 2. 19-20), Zipporah flew to the well and returned with Moses in her talons. Like Wisdom, possessed from of old by the Egyptians and the Children of the East, she dwelt at the bottom of the sea. Another Lilithian sea-creature, Rahab the Harlot, whose family wrought fine linen and who had lain with all the rulers of the world, married Joshua. She thus became ancestress of eight priests and prophets including Hulda the prophetess, which also happens to be one of the names of the Teutonic goddess of the underworld and of witches. Lilith even succeeded in seducing the prophet Elijah without his knowledge, and had a child by him. This may link her to the Shunamite woman, who alone knows the hiding-place of the invisible spirit of Elijah on Mount Carmel, where he waits for a second coming like Arthur and Barbarossa. The Order of Our Lady of Mount Carmel, founded on the mountain in 1154 by St Berthold and a group of Frankish hermits, claims continuity with and spiritual descent from Elijah and the sons of the prophets. Carmelite churches are not infrequently associated with the cult of the Black Virgin.

It is not only in the Jewish esoteric tradition that Lilith sometimes appears in a favourable light. The Gnostic Mandaeans, whose origins are not Christian but stem from John the Baptist, and who have practised their religion uninterruptedly for two thousand years in the swamps of the Tigris-Euphrates delta, know of her from their sacred book, the Ginza. In it Lilith-Zahriel is the daughter of the King and Queen of the Underworld whom they give in marriage to the King of Light, Manda d'Hayye ('knowledge of life'), the personification of Gnosis, or to his son. As a dowry to this marriage of heaven and hell, Lilith brings a magic mirror, a crown and a pearl. She instructs her husband in the secrets of darkness and presents him with a son who combines the wisdom of both realms. When Kushta, the way incarnate, tests him with hard questions, the son defends his mother against charges of being a child-stealing demoness to reveal her as a beneficent spirit who comes to the help of women in labour, sitting on their bed to comfort them.

Lilith has other, less direct, links with John the Baptist in the surprising setting of the Pyrenees, through the characters in the New Testament who most resemble her, Salome and her mother, Herodias. After they had engineered the execution of John, they were exiled along with Herod the Tetrarch, according to Josephus, to Ludgdunum (Convenarum) 'near Spain', now St Bertrand de Comminges (qv). Salome drowned while crossing a frozen river, but Herodias lived on in legend to become identified in the Middle Ages with Diana Nocticula, or Noctiluca, queen of the night-hags. She led her covens to midnight sabbaths where children were sacrificed in fields of wild flax, to be devoured, regurgitated and replaced in their cradles. Perhaps Salome and Herodias are the two Ethiopian maids of the Virgin Mary, Tarbis and Lorda, who founded the cities of Tarbes and Lourdes. Their memory may also have inspired the tradition of a Queen of Ethiopia who, defeated in a war with Moses, fled to exile by the waters of the Adour. According to yet another tale, Lourdes derived its name from the Arab commander of the last stronghold north of the Pyrenees to hold out against Charlemagne. In 778, Rorice II, Bishop of Le Puy (qv), persuaded the general, Mirat, to accompany him on a pilgrimage to the Black Virgin of Mt Anis, where he was baptised Lorus and made governor of the citadel, now renamed Lourdes in his honour.

Lilithian traditions seem to have lingered on in the Pyrenees until the twentieth century. Denis Saurat relates in *La Religion des Géants* that, as recently as 1900, groups of eight to ten girls, roaming in the mountains of the Haute-Ariège, would seize and overpower any unknown young man they chanced upon and use him for their amorous purposes until they decided to release him. Black Pyrenean fairies had a similar reputation.

LAMIAS AND SPHINXES

With the advent of the patriarchy, the dethroning of the great goddesses occurred throughout the ancient world. There are, therefore, many parallels, western and eastern, in addition to those already mentioned, to the negative, raging, demoniac Lilith. Lamia, the name used for her in the Septuagint version of the Bible, was originally a bisexual Libyan queen, daughter of Belus, beloved by Jupiter, who was robbed of her children by jealous Juno. The only offspring who survived was the sea monster, Scylla, guardian of the Straits of Messina, who could devour six men at a time through the wolves' heads that formed her loins. Lamia's own name means both 'gluttonous' and 'lecherous'. Lamia was probably the Libyan version of the Egyptian goddess, Neith, similar to Athene and Anath. She joined a gang of Empusas, shrieking bogey-women who ate their lovers, though retaining her own speciality of enticing and devouring young children. Libya was the early Greek name for the continent of Africa, and the Libyan Sibyl, depicted with her sisters on the marble floor of Siena Cathedral, is the only one shown as black. Lamias later became a separate species, beautiful women who were serpents from the waist down, and in the Middle Ages were synonymous with witches. Keats's poem *Lamia* describes how one such creature returned Melusine-like to her serpent form on her wedding night. That Lamia was also able to bestow wisdom is suggested by her power to pluck out and replace her eyes at will like the triple Graiae whose eye enabled Perseus to find Medusa. Robert Graves observes in this connection that her removable eyes 'may be deduced from a picture of the goddess about to bestow mystic sight on a hero by proffering him an eye.'

Of the various composite monsters in the ancient world known as sphinx (=strangler), that of Egypt was a symbol of Ra's kingship. Later sphinxes were female or hermaphrodite riddlers with animal attributes who carried off boys and youths to satisfy their lust or, like Valkyries, hovered round the scene of fatal combats. Lilith herself is shown as a mixture of wolf, lion and scorpion. Sirens, Rhine-maidens, mermaids, undines, nixies, the fairy Melusine and other water-nymphs tempt voyagers from their path and underline the fatality of desire. Gorgons and basilisks kill at a glance. The Harpies, fierce, starved-looking winged demonesses, of whom one is called 'Darkness', are, like Lilith, associated with storms and pollute everything they touch, emitting an atrocious stench, while the Furies, daughters of earth, pursue men vengefully and drive them mad. There are many dragons, dracs, wouivres (wyverns, vipers), including the Tarasque (cf. Tarascon) and the Graouly (cf. Metz) as well as the lizards of Moulins and Paris, to be found near to Black Virgin sites. They generally symbolize pagan religion and particularly the presence of a goddess and priestesses.

INANNA

To become acquainted with the goddess before she was demoted and demonized, we must return to the writings of the third millennium BC, in that cradle of civilization that was Sumeria. There Inanna was an universal goddess of the heavens, fertility, war, justice, sexual love and healing, whose throne was the world-tree and who bestowed the kingship on the mortal of her choice. When the hero, Gilgamesh, cut down her tree, and the sky-god, Enlil, dispossessed her, she became a homeless wanderer, like Lilith, the Shekinah of the exile, and like Jesus himself.

The bird has its nesting place, but I — my young are dispersed.
The fish lies in calm waters, but I — my resting place exists not,
The dog kneels at the threshold, but I — I have no threshold.

Surely Matthew 8.20 echoes this: 'Foxes have holes, and birds of the air have nests; but the Son of Man has nowhere to lay his head.' Inanna's resemblance to the Christian saviour does not end here. She descended into hell to attend the funeral of the raging bull of heaven, her instrument for terrorizing the earth. In the underworld she was stripped, humiliated, whipped and hung on a peg. On the third day the deities of the upper world became aware of her plight and Enki, the god of waters and wisdom, engineered her release. When she returned to the world of light she had assimilated something of the power of Ereshkigal, the queen of the dead, who may represent Inanna's own occult qualities. One of these powers was that of killing with a glance. In psychological terms this motif may denote the quality of objective discrimination so essential to a woman's integration of her masculine element.

KALI

Inanna is the precursor of Ishtar, Astarte, Aphrodite, and Venus, goddesses whose powers are more specialized than hers. All now belong to the archaeology of myth, save the Venus of astrology. There is one contemporary of Inanna's still active today, however, who retains her awesome cultic power, and that is Kali, goddess of time. The Aryan invaders of north-west India no doubt encountered dark goddesses among the Dravidians of the Indus Valley, whose advanced civilization may have been related to that of the Sumerian Chaldaeans. It now seems probable that reed ships plied between Mesopotamia and India from the beginning of this period, so it would not be surprising if some cross-cultural, iconographical similarities should exist between Indian goddesses and those of the Middle East. One of Kali's names, as the first manifestation of being, is Lalita and Lilith returns the compliment when she acknowledges that Kali is one of her fourteen names. The philological evidence relates the Lilith stem to words of licking, swallowing, lechery and darkness, all consistent with the myth of Kali. Dark, sensuous lilac is derived from the Persian word for midnight blue indigo, itself an import from the Indus. It may carry echoes of the Hindu goddess Lila, whose name means 'play', consort of the blue Vishnu as Narayana, the primal being, moving in the waters.

According to Plutarch, there is also a mountain in India called Lilaeus which produces a black stone known as clitoris, with which the inhabitants of the country adorn their ears (see Pertoka p.25).

NEITH

The most direct influence on the cult and image of the Black Virgin derives without doubt from three goddesses of the ancient Near East, Isis, Cybele and Diana of the Ephesians, but because their influence came through the all-pervading universalism of the later Roman Empire, they will be discussed in the next chapter. There is, however, another goddess from Egypt, who conveys many of the qualities that are inherent in the essential significance of the Black Virgin. Neith was the oldest and wisest of the goddesses, to whom the gods themselves appealed for judgment. Originally the war goddess of Sais, she also presided over the useful arts, a double role which led the Greeks to identify her with Athene. That she was also considered a universal goddess similar to Isis is attested by the inscription on her temple which proclaimed: 'I am all that has been, that is, and that will be. No mortal has yet been able to lift the veil which covers me.' Her epithet, 'the Libyan', links her to the west, traditional home of Lamia and of the dead whose protectress she is. As well as guarding coffins and canopic jars, she is also patroness of marriage. A school of medicine called 'The House of Life' was attached to her sanctuary. She wears a red crown, whose name, 'Net', is in fact her own. As Nut she is the dark, star-studded night sky, arching over the earth, forming with her hands and feet the gateways to life and death. She was the primal androgyne, a self-fertilizing virgin bringing forth life from herself before all worlds. Her crossed arrows represent not merely her warlike nature, but the strife between the opposites, spirit and matter, life and death, which forms the framework of mortal destiny. Her other symbol is therefore, appropriately, the shuttle, with which she weaves the fate of individuals and the universe. The French word for shuttle, 'navette', also means incense-boat, and the roll eaten in honour of the Black Virgin of Candlemas in Marseilles. It is, finally, one of the key symbols of

Catharism. Neumann calls Neith a 'goddess of magic and weaving, unborn goddess, originating in herself', and points out that she was worshipped with mysteries and lantern processions' as are the Black Virgin of Marseilles and many of her sisters. Sir Wallis Budge writes of her as 'the personification of the eternal feminine principle of life which was self-sustaining and self-existent and was secret and unknown and all-pervading'.

ANATH

In her settlement of the dispute between the gods, Neith's judgment was that Horus, despite his youth, should be awarded the throne, while Set, diabolical deity of storm and desert, should be compensated with twice his existing property and two wives. They were the Syrian goddesses, Astarte, parallel to Ishtar, Innana, Aphrodite and Venus, and Anath, very similar to Neith herself and to Athene. Like other Near Eastern goddesses Anath unites within her being opposing qualities — virginal and whorish, maternal and destructive. With her sickle she cuts off the life of Mot, the harvest-god, El's favourite son, whom she grinds in her mill. Baal is her son, brother, lover and also, probably, her victim. One of her names is Qadesh, Holy, which she shares with the forest in which Baal met his death in a struggle with wild bulls. The ass, an animal associated with Set and Lilith, is sacrificed to her. The reborn Baal becomes her son-consort Aleyin or Amurra (Lord of the West).

The Syrian goddesses with their licentious rites were a constant temptation to monotheistic Jewish worshippers of the male god Yahweh. Geoffrey Ashe states that apostate Jews in Egypt at the time of Jeremiah worshipped divine wisdom in the form of the mighty virgin Anath. A stele of the cult under Rameses II, the Pharaoh of the Exodus, refers to her as 'Queen of Heaven and mistress of all the gods'. Jewish mercenaries stationed at Elephantiné near Aswan in the fifth century BC had a temple to Anath as well as one to Yaho (Yahweh). Thus she was associated to the Lord as a female companion, much as Christ and Mary Magdalene were to be linked by the Gnostics of Alexandria. Desmond Stewart argues that it was in this milieu that Jesus grew to manhood, and that the temple where he debated with the elders was at Leontopolis, between Cairo and Alexandria, rather than Jerusalem. Jeremiah (7.8; 44.15-19) complains of the libations and sacrifices of incense and cakes (navettes?) offered to the Queen of Heaven. Epiphanius 850 years later inveighed against assemblies of silly women called Collyridians who worshipped Mary as Queen of Heaven and offered bread rolls (*kollyrida* = cakes of bread) to her throne.

Anath comes nearer to home as a possible direct predecessor of at least one Black Virgin, La Daurade of Toulouse, believed to have been originally a statue of Pallas Athene, the Greek Anath, whose legend becomes linked to that of the web-footed Queen of the South, La Reine Pédauque. Gerard de Sède considers that the most probable prototype for this figure is Anath, hellenized as Aphrodite Anaxerete (queen of virtue). Anaxerete was a lady of Cyprus at whose door her unsuccessful suitor, Iphis, hanged himself, as she looked out, unmoved, from her window. Aphrodite turned her to stone and the resulting statue was known as Venus Prospiciens (looking forwards or out). De Sède states that Anath was a goddess of fertilizing waters, though this function belonged especially to her Persian equivalent, Anahita, goddess of sacred prostitution, whose cult became assimilated to that of Cybele and of Ephesian Artemis. La Reine Pédauque is credited with building the aqueduct which supplied Toulouse with water. According to de Sède, Venus Anaxarete or Anate was turned into a duck, for which the Latin stem is *anat-*. *Nassa* is one Greek word for duck, while the word for queen is *anassa*, a *jeu de mots* which makes Anat a likely candidate for La Reine Pédauque if, like the Celts, we do not differentiate too finely the goose from the duck. Finally de Sède quotes a poem from Ras Shamra which refers obliquely to Anat as Queen of the South, and mentions a medieval planisphere on which Gallina, a Latin name for Venus Anate, is shown as a goddess with her webbed foot on the winter solstice, i.e. the south. Gallina, the hen, would have feet similar to the Lilith of the Burney relief. It may be worth noting that Queen Austris of Toulouse was a Visigoth and that the Old High German for duck is *anut*.

Anath belongs to that widespread category of goddesses whose names contain the syllable 'an', which generally signifies nourishment and abundance, though it can have dark, sinister, devouring connotations. In Christianity there is St Anne, the grandmother of God. Nanna, a child's word for grandmother, is also the Greek word for aunt, an epithet for Cybele and the name of the wife of the dying god, Baldur, who goes to the pyre with him. Anus in Latin means 'old woman' as well as fundament, changing to 'nonna' in Vulgar Latin, from which our word 'nun' derives. As the old gods and goddesses declined into fairy-tale characters Anath, no doubt, turned into Mother Goose, the kindly nanny who soothes the nursery in the telling of tales, though her other side may appear as the wicked stepmother or godmother.

HATHOR

The fairy godmothers of the Egyptians, seven or nine in number, were known as Hathors and they appeared at a birth to prophesy the baby's fate for good or ill. Hathor herself, whom the Greeks identified with Aphrodite, was a sky goddess, Hat-Hor, 'the dwelling of Horus', within whom the sun-god resided. She was, like the cat-goddess, Bast, the bestower of joy and love, the celestial cow who nourished all living creatures with her milk, including the Pharaoh. She was even more solicitous for the dead as guardian of the Theban necropolis (cf. Arles, Marseilles, et al.) and shares with Neith the title 'Queen of the West'. In the last epoch of Egypt, so much did she cherish the dead that the person who had died became known as a Hathor rather than an Osiris. She was sometimes known as 'the Lady of the Sycamore' from the tree on the edge of the desert from which she would welcome souls on their way to the other world with gifts of bread and water. The sycamore, many-breasted with figs, is the Egyptian tree of life which gives forth a milky substance. Hathor shares it as a symbol with Nut, Diana of the Ephesians and with Zacchaeus/St Amador (who climbed one and received there an invitation to entertain Jesus to dinner). This story is told only by St Luke, but it seems to refer to the same occasion as that at which Mary anointed the feet of the Lord and wiped them with her hair. As well as a tree, Hathor was, like Lilith, the ladder on which the righteous could ascend to heaven. She was well-known on the Red Sea coast of Somalia, which may itself be the land of Punt which was originally her home, and that, in some versions, of the Queen of Sheba. She is also known as the Lady of Byblos, the city where the coffin of Osiris, enclosed within a tree after being washed ashore, was made the pillar of a temple. At Byblos she was a serpent-goddess whose cobra symbolized the eye of wisdom.

SEKHMET

The negative aspect of Hathor, the blazing, destructive sun eye of Ra has, like Cybele, Artemis, Medusa, Lilith and St Mary of Egypt, the lion as her symbol. She is, however, more bloodthirsty than any other warrior goddess of Europe and the Near East, a lion-headed deity who boasts 'When I slay men my heart rejoices.' She would have destroyed the race completely in a vengeful rage had not Ra diverted her by placing seven thousand vessels of beer and pomegranate juice on the battlefield, which Sekhmet, mistaking for blood, swallowed up until drunkenness overcame her. Her lion's head she shares with Aion, the time and destiny which devour all things, the wrath of God that is the working of the law of cause and effect. The Sphinx, too, is a lion, who kills the man that lacks the Gnosis to answer her questions about the nature and meaning of human life. Some modern astrologers see Saturn, the dark tester and teacher of wisdom, as an essentially feminine influence.

Isha Schwaller de Lubicz, analysing the etymology of Sekhmet, describes it as the personification of the chaotic darkness which brings light out of ignorance. Since Sekhmet symbolizes the putrefaction without which the spiritual life-force cannot be released at death, we may call her, like Kali, the merciful. Lubicz also depicts her as a sort of telluric lightning-conductor, attracting to itself the fire of Ptah and neutralizing it. From the interaction of these forces, the Egyptian Prometheus, Nefertum, arose. Sekhmet is the annihilating power which makes conception possible: one form must die before another can come into being. The beloved in the 'Song of Solomon' is black because she has been exposed to the sun. St Mary the Egyptian suffered the same fate from her long life of penance in the desert and, at death, a lion dug her grave. One of the reasons given for the blackness of our virgins is that Mary, too, was very

sunburnt. The most important function of the Black Virgin is her
power to stay the destructive hand of God, tempering justice
with mercy.

Once upon a time, God's dove and God's raven were
sundered, and the raven of the Ark became accursed. It, like the
dove, had once been white and was blackened in performance of
its Promethean role of bringing the light and fire of consciousness to mankind. Marie-Louise von Franz describes the raven as
the light-bringer *par excellence*, the creative depression which is
God's messenger. The process, however depressing it may seem,
is the way.

CHAPTER 2
The classical tradition

In the first three centuries of the Christian era it seemed increasingly as though a generalized worship of the Great Goddess might establish itself as the dominant religion of the Roman Empire, incorporating even the cults of Mithra and the Unconquered Sun. Under a multitude of names she had held sway from east to west before the Hellenes arrived in Greece or the Romans in Italy. Now, despite the formalities of emperor-worship and official religion, a wave of popular devotion was sweeping her back into the pre-eminence she had enjoyed before the Olympian dispensation. There is a tendency for all the goddesses to merge into each other, which makes it difficult to be sure which qualities to attribute to which divinity. The process of merging accelerated during the period we shall be looking at. In Christianity the feminine principle was represented by Black Virgins, White Virgins and a host of female saints, each having her own symbol and specific nature. As Christianity gradually asserted itself, the great bronze and marble statues of the pagan deities were destroyed. Smaller, household images or votive offerings, hidden in the earth, in cleft rocks or hollow trees, survived, especially in remote country places. Some were lost, some, perhaps, still visited as fairy trees and stones, long after their true nature had been forgotten. The memory of them may have influenced a later generation of religious sculptors. In addition, at the time of the Crusades, original pagan statues, or images based on them, were brought back from the east by returning warriors, as Madonnas.

Apart from the candle-smoke theory, this is the simplest and most widely held explanation for the existence of Black Virgins in Europe. They would thus be a survival, and a continuation under a new name and a new religion of goddesses from the classical world. Of the multitudes of candidates available, three stand out by reason of their popularity in the Europe of late paganism and from the fact that each has at some time been represented as black: Artemis, Isis and Cybele. The first to arrive was Artemis.

ARTEMIS — IN ARCADIA

It is debatable how far the Artemis of Greece, the 'maiden huntress', should be identified with the many-breasted, fertile, Ephesian goddess. Between them they combine the paradox of virgin and mother which is at the heart of Christian Marian dogma. In pre-Hellenic times Artemis was universally worshipped in Greece, her name being commonly derived from *artamos,* slaughterer, a fact which provides a possible link with those Black Virgins who have special affinities with the guild of butchers (cf. Murat). As huntress she both preserves and destroys game animals, but she does not draw the line at animals. Human sacrifice, real or simulated, was offered to her, and she herself has a bloodthirsty record of killing her would-be lovers, or those of her nymphs. When Orion, the mighty hunter and beautiful giant touched her indiscreetly during the chase, she summoned up the great scorpion from the earth to despatch him. In another version she draws her silver bow and shoots him through the head as he swims towards her. This suggests she is a head-hunter, too, like Kali and, perhaps, also, like the Black Virgin of Einsiedeln, who stands atop the skull of St Meinrad. Although Artemis seems to have disliked all males, she particularly resisted heroes of the stamp of Hercules and Achilles.

The fate of Actaeon, who came too close to her and was subsequently torn to pieces by his own hounds, is well-known. In yet another tale, mistaking her for a bear, she slew her beloved other half, Callisto, the wolfish Lycaon's daughter, after she had yielded to the embraces of Zeus in the temple where he was worshipped in wolf form. Before Callisto died, however, the nymph bore a son, Arcas, from whom Arcadia, Artemis' land of predilection, took its name. The authors of *The Holy Blood and the Holy Grail* have pointed out the connection between the wolf tribe of Benjamin and the bear-land of Arcadia. In the first Book of Maccabees, Chapter 12, Jonathan, the High Priest, writes to the Spartans to enlist their help in the struggle against Antiochus Epiphanes. He encloses a letter sent to a previous High Priest (probably Onias I who held office from 323-300 BC) from Areius, King of the Spartans, offering non-military assistance and stating: 'It has been found in writing concerning the Spartans and the Jews that they are brethren and are of the family of Abraham' (v. 21). This may be relevant to our hypothesis that the Merovingian dynasty, a wolf god and the symbol of the bear are all involved in the history of the Black Virgin cult.

ARCADIA AND THE ARK

Many associations can be teased out of the word Arcadia. The Greek word in the Septuagint version of the Bible from Alexandria used *kibitos* for both Noah's Ark and the Ark of the Covenant, though a barge and a box are very different objects. The root word, *kibos*, also yields the diminutive *kiborion*. This is the seed-vessel of the Nile water lily or lotus, as well as our word ciborium, the covered chalice used to contain the eucharistic bread. (For the Ark in which Moses floated on the Nile among the bulrushes a different word is used, though from a more archaic version of the same root.) The name of King Arthur may be derived from the cognate Celtic *arto* meaning a bear, or *art*, a stone. Latin and Greek forms deriving from the radical *arc* include words meaning bow, rainbow, arch, arcane, enclose, coffin, prison, concealed and citadel, and also bear-like, keep safe and keep away. *Dia*, in Greek, is a poetical term for Zeus, and for Hera (she who belongs to Zeus). In Latin 'Dia' is the name of the mother of Mercury. Hermes, the Greek Mercury, is born in Arcadia, in a dark cave on Mt Kyllene, the son of Maia and Zeus. Maia (= midwife) was very close to Callisto, and when the latter was assumed to heaven as the Great Bear, looked after her son, Arcas. One of Maia's names in Rome is Maiesta, meaning majesty (this is a description given by art historians to the great majority of Black Virgins, particularly those to be found in the Auvergne). Maia is goddess of the merry but Virgin month sacred to Venus, Mary and the mercurial Heavenly Twins. When Artemis herself had to be fitted into the new patriarchal scheme on Olympus, it was necessary to assign to her parents, of whom the first are Zeus and Demeter, the Great Mother who was goddess of Greece before Zeus appeared on the scene. This parentage would make her akin to Persephone, the dangerous Virgin goddess of the underworld. In yet another version Persephone herself is the mother of Artemis, thus making the daughter a feminine version of the holy child of Eleusis. Isis and Dionysos are also, somewhat surprisingly, cast in the role of Artemis' parents (though the Bacchic connection appears to have continued in the tradition of ritually sponging with wine the Black Isiac Virgin of Le Puy).

The most generally accepted story of the birth of Artemis, however, is that she was the daughter of Leto, whose name may mean stone or lady, and whose father was Polos, the pole-star or axis of the universe. Leto came to Delos in the form of a she-wolf from Lycis, wolf-land, and brought forth Artemis without pain, a fact which made her, like the Black Virgin of Le Puy, a patron of easy births. A dragon, the Python, had tried to prevent Leto, like the heavenly woman of the Book of Revelation, from giving birth to the sun-god Apollo, who was Artemis' younger twin.

The secret of Artemis, she of the ark and the art, the androgynous product of sun and moon, cannot be confined by time, space or custom. The Ark/Grail is the symbol of the virgin whore, wisdom, who mixes all things in an orgy of syncretism, to bring forth the oneness of truth without diversity.

Robert Graves in *The White Goddess* provides further amplification of the motif 'Ark' that lends some weight to this proposition. He tells of the Roman Emperor, Alexander Severus (AD 222-235), the Arkite, born in the Temple of Alexander the Great at Arka in Lebanon. He developed his own syncretistic Arkite religion in which Abraham, Orpheus, Alexander and Jesus Christ were household gods.

Earlier Arkites, mentioned in Genesis 10.17 — a passage which contains a mention of Nimrod, who is the Old Testament Orion, and of several peoples connected with Saba — were worshippers of Astarte/Ishtar, the goddess to whom an acacia-wood ark was sacred. For the Jews the Ark of the Lord, also made of acacia wood, contained the most sacred objects and became itself the most sacred object, symbol of the Shekinah, God's presence among his people. To touch or approach the Ark is death, but acacia symbolizes resurrection and immortality. Some say the son of Solomon and the Queen of Saba/Sheba took the Ark to Ethiopia, others that it remained hidden in the Temple in Jerusalem. The acacia from which it is built is an incorruptible and ardent plant, which reveals, in masonic ritual, the tomb of Hiram, the Master Builder of the Temple, the one who holds the secret of the lost arcane tradition. The tomb depicted in Poussins's *Les Bergers d'Arcadie*, believed by many to point to secrets of the Merovingian blood-line, is in old Plantard territory near Rennes-le-Château, at Arques (see Paris 1). Could the other name for Poussin's pinating, *Et in Aracadia ego*, which is also the motto of the Plantard family, mean, in addition to the obvious translation, 'And in the Ark I am the God/Goddess'? Might we even guess that Joan of Arc, Art or Aix, friend of René d'Anjou of the Prieuré, an Artemisian warrior-maiden, inspired by a fairy tree and a devotee of Black Virgins, is somehow involved in the mystery?

Artemis of Ephesus

It is with Artemis of Ephesus rather than the Arcadian Lady of Wild Things that we must now concern ourselves in the quest for the origins of the Black Virgin. According to legend, she started as a black meteoric stone discovered in a swamp by Amazons. Such a stone, known in French as *bétyle*, from the Greek *baitulos*, both manifests the divine presence and signifies Bethel, the house of God. It was there that Jacob had his dream of the ladder and angels while resting his head on the Stone of Scone which lies beneath the throne of Britain. We may remember here that the Holy Grail is sometimes considered to be a stone, as well as a vessel.

Ephesus was where the Virgin Mary traditionally spent her closing years before her Dormition and Assumption, with St John, before his exile to Patmos. In Ephesus in AD 431 the Virgin Mary was proclaimed 'Mother of God', and her cult spread thence to the city of the she-wolf, Rome, and so to all the corners of the world, as, indeed, a thousand years earlier had that of her predecessor, the Black Ephesian. The best-known image of Artemis of Ephesus, a Roman alabaster and bronze statue of the second century, shows her with black face, hands and feet, multiple breasts, on her head a mural crown or tower, and on her dress images including bulls, goats, deer and a bee. It is probable that the image of the goddess which the Phocaeans brought to Gaul with them in 600 BC, where they founded Massilia, now Marseilles, was not dissimilar, since the cult travelled from there to Rome. Other goddesses were worshipped in Marseilles, but Artemis seems to have held her place in Massiliot hearts as the Lady of the City, which was to become the richest trading emporium of the western Mediterranean. The Phocaeans were great travellers, sailing as far afield as Britain in their quest for tin and other precious goods, and where they went they would no doubt have taken with them images of their patroness (cf. Banyuls). Furthermore, visitors to Marseilles, being impressed by the statues of various goddesses they saw there, may well have taken replicas home with them. It is striking that the greatest incidence of Black Virgins occurs in areas where the Phocaeans had settlements, or important trading partners such as the Arverni of the Auvergne. Thus it is possible that in such regions as Provence, the Rhône, Catalonia and the river valleys of the eastern Pyrenees, a custom may have grown up, during the long centuries of Massiliot influence, of venerating the goddess in her dark aspect.

Artemis and the tree

This face of the night is not always merciful, as we have already glimpsed. Artemis is hostile to love and punishes sexual transgressors severely. Unawakened little girls, brownies playing bears to her honour in the forest, are great favourites of hers, but boys fare less well at the hands of her devotees. In Sparta, youths were flogged in front of the statue of Artemis Orthia (upright), in a combination of fertility rite and painful puberty initiation. The sexual puritanism of the new goddess of Christianity, with its proliferation of monastic establishments based on Marseilles and Lérins from the early fifth century, would not altogether have displeased Arcadian Artemis.

The most notable cultic feature belonging both to Artemis and to the Black Virgins is the fact that they both tend to make their home in trees where they are later 'found'. Artemis Orthia, like the Black Virgin of Bourg, was found in a hollow willow tree, and hence is known as Lygodesma, 'willow-captive'. Other images of her were adored in a myrtle and a cedar. A third-century coin from Myrrha in Asia Minor shows the Virgin in a tree flanked by two axe-wielding figures, possibly Cabiri. From Scherpenheuvel in Belgium to Prats in the Pyrenees, via Chartres and Longpont, there are many examples of Black Virgins being associated with an earlier tree cult. Then too both Artemis and the Black Virgin demand to be worshipped in their own way, where they have been found. When moved against her will the Black Virgin resists by becoming insupportably heavy. Artemis too indicates her disapproval in this way, as when the flagellation of the young Spartans slackened, a phenomenon noted by the priestesses who carried her during the ceremony.

Artemis and the underworld

In her darker, Persephone, side Artemis is often confused and identified with Hecate, an underworld power (Notre-Dame de Sous-Terre), whose sacred trees are the graveyard yew, good for bows and for arrow poison, and the willow, the wicked witch tree. The triple goddess rules in all the worlds, but it is as the invincible Queen of the Dead that she most resembles our Black Virgins. Our Lady of Avioth, found in a hawthorn tree, still preserves outside her basilica a unique architectural feature, La Recévresse, where dead babies were offered to the Black Virgin (Artemis and Hecate both care for babies and bestow a quick death). In Marseilles, amidst the ancient necropolis, Notre Dame de Confession presides in a crypt over the tombs of the martyrs from whom she takes her name. One of these, sometimes met with elsewhere as a companion of Black Virgins, is St Maurice (Maurus = Moorish, black; Maurs = Mars) to whom one prays to be delivered from unwanted parents. Hecate presides over purification rites, so February, month of the dead which begins with Candlemas, the Feast of the Purification of the Blessed Virgin Mary, is especially her time. In 472 this feast succeeded to the torchlight procession in honour of Persephone, and that of the Lupercalia. At this feast a goat and a dog were sacrificed to the wolf-god, and young women were ritually beaten with goat-skin thongs. This tradition continues in our 'beating of the bounds'. The most famous and ancient Candlemas procession is that of St Victor of Marseilles, where the new light is brought up from the crypt with green candles. Candlemas, the oldest feast of the Virgin, also commemorates the presentation of Christ in the

Temple, a second epiphany at the home of divine wisdom. Persephone's name contains, etymologically, not only elements of destruction but of epiphany, the showing forth of the light. Her male equivalent, the Roman god of February purifications, Februus, is a form of Dispater, god of the dead, who, as Pluto, rapes Persephone into the underworld. As Plutus, he is born from Demeter or Irene, Peace (the Black Virgin, Notre-Dame de Paix, in Paris, is compared in 'Horizons Blancs' to a statue of Irene holding Plutus). The companion to the Lady of Candlemas in the Christian calendar, and to the Black Virgin in many of her shrines, is St Roch, shown with a dog at his heels. The dog is also the sacred animal of Hecate, as both devourer of corpses and the guide of souls to the underworld.

Diana, the Artemis/Hecate of the Roman world, the wood-goddess of the golden bough, whose name means 'shining one' or 'dual-Ana' (i.e. the goddess of both earth and moon), is also the feminine form of Dis/Dianus/Janus. She degenerates but persists in the Christian era as the goddess of witches, and queen of the night. Something of her tradition lives on in Black Virgins, making them much prized by modern necromancers. Black Annis/Dana, a Celtic parallel to Diana in her destructive mode, may have given her name to Mont Anis, home of the Black Virgin of Le Puy, but Anis also reminds us of the favourite drink of those who talk the *langue d'oc*, which is made from a flower belonging to the genus artemisia. No wonder St Bernard selected for his first abbey in the valley of light a site by the stream called Absinthe (the 'wormwood' on the sponge at the Crucifixion). The great feast of the Virgin, the Assumption, which occurs on 15 August, probably originates in a festival of Diana. Metz Cathedral (qv) was built on top of a Temple of Diana (see also Calatayud, Manfredonia, Le Puy).

CYBELE

Cybele is the Phrygian mother of the gods whose prototype has been traced back to the neolithic matriarchal civilization of Çatal Hüyük. She was first worshipped as a black stone, and it was thus that she journeyed to Rome in 205 BC, sent by King Attalus of Pergamum at the request of the Senate. It had been advised in the Sibylline Books that only she could save them from the showers of stones and the inroads of Hannibal that beset them. She was carried by matrons to the Palatine site of what was to be the Virgin of the Ara Coeli (qv), and placed in the Temple of Victory. Annually, on 25 March, the Christian Lady Day, her statue, whose head consisted of a black stone, was bathed in the River Almo (Almus = nourishing, cf. Alma Mater). To the Romans she was simply 'Magna Mater', the Great Mother, and the earliest Phrygian name for her consort was Papas, father, which is still the Greek word for priest. In Pessinus, the black stone, which in Rome became the head of the goddess, was considered to be her throne. Can it have been a memory of this tradition that led Hincmar, the ninth-century Archbishop of Rheims, to assert that the appropriate colour for the throne of the Virgin was black? The name Pessinus, though presumably from the old Phrygian language, awakens echoes surprisingly relevant to the significance of Cybele through the only two Greek words with the root *pess*. *Pessos* is an oval stone especially used in playing draughts, a cubic mass of building, the dark edge of the pupil of the eye, and a pessary. *Pesso* means to bake, ripen, ferment or digest.

By the third century AD Cybele was the supreme deity of Lyons, capital of the three Gauls, where a Black Virgin cult flourishes today. Julian the Apostate favoured her cult and composed a beautiful prayer in which he apostrophized her as the Virgin: 'Wisdom, Providence, Creator of our souls'. Bulls were sacrificed to her at the Vatican in the last years of the fourth century and, as late as 410 AD she was still publicly honoured in Gaul. Originally a mountain goddess, generally accompanied by lions, she became the tutelary deity of cities and frontier citadels, protecting her people from war and pestilence, and speaking to them in subterranean oracles and ecstasies. Her name is etymologically linked with the words for crypt, cave, head and dome and is distantly related to the Ka'aba, the cube-shaped holy of holies in Mecca that contains the feminine black stone venerated by Islam. Her youthful companion was the lesser consort-god, Attis, who was castrated and transformed into the pine-tree. In his memory and to honour the goddess, her priests, the Galli, were also eunuchs.

The word Galli, which also means Gauls (and those Gallic birds, cocks), reminds us that Phrygia was invaded and partly occupied in 278 BC by Gauls who called their new homeland

Galatia. The Gauls had reservations about a castrated god but, being accustomed to the worship of the goddess, were not slow to welcome Cybele, and assimilate her into their own divinities of water, fertility and victory. She was worshipped from the fourth century BC at Ra, which became Les Saintes Maries de la Mer, along with her sisters and rivals Artemis and Isis. Examples of the Black Virgin sites that have been associated with her include Aix-en-Provence, where her consort has become St Mitra, and Madrid, where she presides from her chariot in the famous fountain over the traffic of the Plaza de Cibeles in the capital of the bull cult. (See also Agde, on the Golf du Lion, Arles, Auxerre, Avignon, Beaune, Chartres, Clermont-Ferrand, Grande-Chartreuse, Laon, Limoux, Marseilles, Mauriac, Mézières, Mont St Michel, Monte Vergine, Patti/Tindari, Périgueux, Rocamadour, Rome, Tarascon, Toulouse, Tournai, Valence/Cornas, Vence/St Paul and Vichy.)

Lyons, city of Cybele

Although her cult was slow to establish pre-eminence there, the city of Cybele in France is without doubt Lyons, where her huge temple (86 by 53 metres) has been supplanted by the great basilica of Notre Dame de Fourvière (the old forum) and the oratory of the Black Virgins. Her lion is still on the arms of the city surmounting three fleur de lys. Of the cult of Cybele little now remains at Lyons; the foundations of the temple have been excavated; the mask of the statue of the goddess with red hair, and her altar, are preserved in the magnificent Musée de la Civilisation Gallo-Romaine; the bust of Tutela, protectress of cities who holds a horn of plenty, is probably an aspect of her; the rue du Boeuf may commemorate the crowned bull led in procession on her great feast. In AD 177 the coincidence of her feast of Hilaria, 25 March (Lady Day) with the Christian Good Friday was the cause of public rioting and the repression of the Christian community. It is curious in this connection that at Le Puy (qv) whenever Lady Day and Good Friday coincide, a jubilee is declared, to which pilgrims flock from all nations.

An interesting souvenir of Cybele persisted in Lyons until the sixteenth century in the form of a statue of the goddess Copia (Abundance) in the Church of St Etienne, where on Christmas night (the Vigil of St Stephen), women presented candles and offerings of fruit and animals to the goddess, and departed walking backwards. The local name for the statue was Ferrabo, believed to be a corruption of Farrago, a word meaning a mixture of different grains in a hotch-potch, an excellent description of Lyons, city of Cybele where so many traditions meet. According to Saillens the cult of the Black Virgin of Fourvière dates from the destruction of this idol from the pagan past.

We do not know for certain the colour of the original Virgin of Fourvière, destroyed by the Huguenots in 1562, but Louis XI, whose predilection for Black Virgins is well known, stated that he had always had from his earliest youth a 'great affection for the glorious Virgin Mary, mother of God, and for her chapel of Fourvière on the mount of Lyons'. He spent five months in the city in 1476, between two pilgrimages to Le Puy. His first gesture was to climb up to the shrine and make an offering to Our Lady, whom he endowed richly with the town of Charlieu and 84 parishes.

In the year AD 186, during the golden age of Gallo-Roman Lyons, on Fourvière, Julia Domna, known as the philosopher, second wife of the Emperor Septimius Severus, gave birth to the Emperor Caracalla. Syrian, and initiate of Astarte, she was a passionate disciple of Apollonius of Tyana, a contemporary of Jesus, who died at a great age, in Ephesus (like John). His life's work included a syncretistic and esoteric missionary journey to Babylon, Persia, Alexandria, the source of the Nile, Spain and Provence, purifying the rites of all the shrines he visited. Of his books on *Sacrifices*, *Astrological Predictions* and *Pythagoras* (whose successor he was considered), almost nothing has survived, and he himself, unjustly accounted a rival to the Christian God, has faded on the palate of history.

The Christian church in Lyons prided itself on its own direct link to the Ephesus of St John through Irenaeus, its second bishop, who complained of the many foolish women attracted to Gnosticism in the Rhône Valley. He was a pupil of that Polycarp who, according to Irenaeus, 'had intercourse with John'. He probably died in the destruction of Lyons by Septimius Severus in 197. The relics of the first bishop Potinus, martyred after the quarrel with the followers of Cybele in 177, were thrown into the Rhône along with those of his fellow martyrs, but it seems likely that they were commemorated in the church of the Maccabees on the plateau of Sarra, which it shared with the church of St Irenaeus. This highly unusual name for a Christian church is that of the Old Testament apocryphal book in which mention is made of the link between Israel and Sparta (Arcadia).

In the Church of the Maccabees was venerated the body of a fourth-century Archbishop, St Justus, who retired to the ruins of Thebes to lead a cenobitic existence amid the remnants of Egyptian syncretism. From the Thebaid, monasticism spread to Marseilles with Cassian. The district of St Just is now next to that of St Luc, who might be expected to be a favourite of the Lyonnais, given the similarity of his name to that of Lug, their divine founder.

The Maccabees yielded place to the monastery of St Just where Clement V was crowned Pope on 14 November 1305. As he and King Philippe le Bel were passing in procession by the convent of La Madeleine, a huge block of masonry detached itself from the building, killing the Pope's brother and the Duke of Brittany and narrowly missing pontiff and monarch. It was this king, with the reluctant collusion of the Pope, who brought about the destruction of the Templars in 1307-8. Their quarter in Lyons, a veritable forbidden city, was larger than that of Paris, and may have been the heart of the mercantile operations of the whole order. The Templars might still be here today if they had heeded the recommendations of the Council of Lyons in 1274, at which Pope Gregory X proposed a merger with the Knights of St John. He also tried to reunite the Churches of East and West by reforming the morals of the clergy and liberating the Holy Land. The first of these aims was realised in twentieth-century Lyons in the form of the Orthodox Catholic Church founded in 1939 at 16 rue du Boeuf by Fr Kovalewsky who rejected the Great Schism. The Liberal Catholic Church, an off-shoot of the Theosophical Society, which said Mass in French and believed, like Apollonius of Tyana, in reincarnation, also flourished in Lyons between the wars, despite excommunication. Another heresy, that of 'the poor men of Lyons', which claimed to preserve a pure and uncorrupted pre-Constantinian Christianity, was founded in the city in the twelfth century and still survives in the Piedmont across the border from the Black Virgins of Modane and St Martin de Vésubie.

That Lyons is a city of occultism, Templars, Tarot and heresy cannot be laid at the door of the Black Virgins of Fourvière or that of their neighbour, Cybele. Yet Lyons is also a city, where, despite the depradations of the past two thousand years, nothing is forgotten. In the painting by the nineteenth-century artist Orsel in the basilica, Mary is shown enthroned in the sky, saving her city of Lyons just discernible below. Under her throne a lion is lying.

Lionesses lick their cubs into shape and life. One of the endearing features which various Black Virgins share with Cybele Fatua is to help infants to speak, to awaken the word in them. Then, too, as a lioness protects her cubs, Our Lady of Victories and Cybele/Andarta fight for their cities and protect them against the foe. Cybele, as Fortune, also brings peace and prosperity between wars. A second-century BC relief from Rome shows her enthroned, stately and matronly, looking for all the world like the later Queen Victoria, holding a shield like Britannia, being drawn on a processional cart by two lions. In this matriarchal role she is very much the confidante of women, reflecting the present and the future in a comforting light, Our Lady of Perpetual Succour and Good Hope. It is however in her initiatory aspect as sibylline hierophant of the mysteries of death and rebirth, whether her youthful consort be Attis, Dionysus or Mithra, that her influence on the cult of the Black Virgin is of greatest interest to modern votaries.

ISIS

The Prieuré, as we have noted, insist that the Black Virgin, whether worshipped under other names, such as Diana or Cybele, is in fact Isis, the true goddess of France, now known as Our Lady of Light. Some 500 years before Dagobert II reputedly set about restoring the cult of the Black Virgin she had already, in *The Golden Ass* of Apuleius, claimed to be *the* universal goddess, subsuming the attributes of all the others.

> 'I am Nature, the universal Mother, mistress of all the elements, primordial child of time, sovereign of all things spiritual, queen of the dead, queen also of the immortals,

the single manifestation of all gods and goddesses that are.
. . . The primeval Phrygians call me Pessinuntica [i.e.
Cybele], Mother of the gods; the Athenians, sprung from
their own soil, call me Cecropian Artemis; for the islanders
of Cyprus I am Paphian Aphrodite; for the archers of
Crete I am Dictynna, for the trilingual Sicilians, Stygian
Proserpine [Persephone]: and for the Eleusinians their
ancient Mother of the Corn [Demeter].

'Some know me as Juno, some as Bellona of the Battles;
others as Hecate, others again as Rhamnusia [Nemesis?],
but both races of Aethiopians, whose lands the morning
sun first shines upon, and the Egyptians who excel in
ancient learning and worship me with ceremonies proper
to my god-head, call me by my true name, namely, Queen
Isis.' (trans. Robert Graves.)

So how are we to differentiate Isis from all the other goddesses
she assimilates? She tells Lucius one thing he must do in order to
be saved and become human. While her priests offer her the first
fruits of the new sailing season by dedicating a ship to her, he
must follow the High Priest and eat some blooms from the
bouquet of roses attached to his sistrum. Here she associates
herself with the rose, though she shares that symbol with
Aphrodite, her indigenous flower being rather the lotus, or Nile
water-lily, that rises from mud through water to reflect the sun.
The other symbol, the boat, is also the prerogative of Aphrodite
as protectress of sailors, but the barque of Isis bears more
explicit connotations such as that of caring for the dead on their
night-sea journey. In her care for Osiris she tends all the dead,
but she also nurtures the living. More than any other goddess,
Isis is shown as a nursing mother, with the infant Horus at her
breast or the infant Harpocrates on her lap, enjoining silence,
though she also suckles Pharaohs, as the Black Virgins of
Chartres and Châtillon granted their milk to Fulbert and
Bernard. In these images lie the origins of Madonna and Child.
The ankh which Isis carries as supreme initiatrix may account
for some of the oddly shaped sceptres carried by the Black
Virgins who, like Isis, often favour the colour green. Their
greenness and blackness point to the beginning of the opus
whose secret, according to alchemists, is to be found in 'the sex

of Isis'. As the whore wisdom, she spent ten years in a brothel in Tyre. She alone knows the secret name of the god Ra, through which she wields her power. Her own name is considered by many scholars to mean 'throne', while to others, when combined with Maat, it signifies 'ancient wisdom'. Every living being is a drop of her blood, to be protected under her wings in death and lovingly restored to life. Though the greatest danger to the Church, she has never entirely lost her popularity and prestige in the west. Diana is the queen of the night for witches, Isis for Masons and Rosicrucians. Of the great Black Virgin cities of France, Lyons is devoted to Cybele, the patroness of Marseilles is Artemis. Toulouse of Pallas Athene in its very essence *is* the Queen of the South, home of a Gnostic wisdom school in the sixth century. It was left to Paris, eventually the greatest of them all, to be selected by Isis, greatest of the goddesses, as her sacred capital.

Isis in Paris

There are many etymologies of the name 'Paris'. Its older name, 'Lutetia', has been derived from Lucus, the descendant of Noah who became a Celtic king, but also from the Greek word for light and from Lug/Luc, the god of light who lent his name to Lyons and other Celtic cities. It has even been derived from mud.

Hercules, on his way from Asia Minor to the garden of the Hesperides, was accompanied by some Parrhesians who abandoned the journey to settle on the Seine, where they became the Parisii, the ruling clan of the area. Of the Parrhesians little is known, but a clue as to their true identity may be found in the Greek word *parrhesia,* which means frankness. There was also a fourth-century BC Ephesian painter, Parrhesius, who accorded royal honours to himself and whose paintings of divinities on wood and paper became, like those of St Luke, models for later artists. It is to the Franks, however, that we must once again return. Like the founders of Rome and London, they claimed descent from Troy through Francion, son of Hector. Paris, the new capital, simply commemorates their unfortunate countryman, who, in the beauty contest of the three goddesses, awarded the golden apple to Aphrodite, and later abducted Helen, sparking off the Trojan war. The Franks, profligate with clues to their origin, would have arrived in Paris via Troyes.

Another etymology stresses the importance of the syllable 'is', a pre-Celtic word for a holy place where there is a subterranean current of water or telluric energy called a wouivre, which creates special conditions favourable for divinatory and initiatory purposes. This sacred syllable may account for the suffix -is or -es to be found in the name of many French towns.

Isis can easily assimilate such diverse explanations within her all-accommodating universality, but that which honours her most is the derivation of Par-Isis, 'grove' or 'barque' of Isis, and the Île de la Cité certainly bears a close resemblance to a Nile felucca. In Roman times her temple was at the western limits of the city, on the marshy left bank of the Seine, later the site of the famous abbey and church of St Germain-des-Prés and of St Sulpice. Some time during this period, Paris was evangelized by Dionysius, St Denis, who is joint male patron of France with St Michael. Donald Attwater writes of Denis that in the ninth century 'a very strange legend had grown up around him in which three different people, living in different ages, were made into one man'. The first, a learned Athenian converted by St Paul, was martyred on Montmartre, hill of Mercury, martyrs or, more prosaically, pine-martens or sables. The second was a sixth-century theologian who wrote three books: *The Celestial Hierarchy*, an account of how the nine choirs of angels mediate God to man, *The Divine Names*, on the attributes of God, and *The Mystical Theology*, which describes the ascent of the soul to God. Denis's great achievement was to synthesize Neo-Platonic thought and Christian dogma. The third St Denis was said in the sixth century to have been sent to Paris in 250, where he was martyred as the first bishop. *En route* he visited the image of the Virgo Paritura, later to become the Black Virgin of Longpont (qv), where he explained to the people that the Virgin had now given birth. After execution he carried his severed head to the site of the present basilica of St Denis.

Another St Dionysius was the great third-century Bishop of Alexandria and head of the Catechetic School there in succession to Origen, who was accused of tritheism by Dionysius of Rome, and tried to reconcile warring factors within the Church. The god Dionysus may also have a part to play in the legend through the sojourn which the third St Denis made in the Faubourg St Jacques, a suburb, where, until the Revolution, there stood a church dedicated to Our Lady of the Vines. A suggested etymology for Jacques is Iacchus, Dionysus as the divine child of the Eleusinian Mysteries, and it is not immediately obvious why it should be a pet-name for John. A pilgrim on the milky way to Santiago de Compostela is also known as a 'jack'.

The cult of St Denis owes much to St Genevieve and the Merovingian dynasty. Between the time of these two saints, Lutetia had enjoyed a brief period as capital of the Roman Empire under Julian the Apostate (332-63) who loved the place, which he saved from the incursions of the Salian Franks. His attempt to restore the cult of King Helios and the Mother of the Gods proved short-lived, as did his effort to keep out the Franks. It would not be long before Paris was turning to them for fear of an even worse fate. Meanwhile they had Genevieve.

She was a shepherdess, like other Arcadian saints, born of a rich family in Nanterre around the year 420. St Germain of Auxerre, *en route* to Britain to combat Pelagianism, met her while she was still a child, foretold her future sanctity and received her vows. Another who recognised her worth was St Marcel, Bishop of Paris, whose feast is on All Saints' Day (1 November), who turned water into wine and delivered the city from a dragon whose lair was in a harlot's tomb. Genevieve lost her parents at fifteen, and went to stay with her godmother in the city. From there she undertook charitable journeys to Meaux, Laon, Tours and Orléans, all of which have been associated with the Black Virgin cult. In 450, when Attila and his Huns were at the gates of Paris, Genevieve stopped the tide of panic by announcing that they would not attack. She was proved right, and, shortly after, they were defeated at the Catalaunian Fields by Aetius, with his mixed army of Gallo-Romans, Franks, Burgundians and Visigoths.

Soon it was the turn of the Franks from Tournai, under their King, Childeric, son of Merovée/Merweg and father of Clovis, to besiege the city. To relieve the starvation of its inhabitants, Genevieve organised and led an armada of ships to Troyes and Arcis (the Is of the Ark, or the Ark of Isis?), which returned laden with corn. When the city eventually fell to the Franks, Childeric did not hold this act of defiance against Genevieve, whose character and sage counsel he much respected. Perhaps his native ferocity had been mitigated by his Thuringian wife Basine who had made him stand outside the door of the palace on their wedding night. During his chaste vigil he had a vision of wolves, bears, lions, leopards and unicorns. Their son, Clovis, the first King of France, and his sainted queen, Clotilda, were friends of Genevieve, and at her behest inaugurated a programme of church-building. The cult of St Denis was especially close to Genevieve's heart. She and Clovis died within a short time of each other in 511 and 512, and were buried close together in the church which became the Pantheon. According to an old custom the reliquary of St Genevieve is never exposed without that of St Marcel.

Clovis was succeeded by Childebert I, 'King of Paris', who brought back with him from an expedition to Toledo the tunic of St Vincent with a number of chalices and vases from the treasure of Solomon. St Germain, Bishop of Paris (494-576), advised him to build a church and abbey worthy to house such relics. The site chosen was that of the old temple of Isis. A black statuette of the goddess, 'slender, tall and upright, naked save for some wisps of garment around her limbs', was venerated as the Virgin in the Church of St Germain-des-Prés until broken up on the orders of Abbot Briconnet in 1514. The Benedictines of St Germain are, like the priests of Isis, 'wearers of the black'. The seal of Abbot Hugh III, 1138, shows her holding what seems to be a long lotus or fleur de lys in her right hand. Today, the Black Virgin is still at St Germain, though hard to find. All the Merovingian kings were buried there until Dagobert I removed the royal mausoleum to St Denis. According to P. Saintyves, the successor to Isis is not only St Genevieve, patroness of Paris, but also St Gudule, patroness of Brussels (qv), present-day capital of what was once the old Frankish kingdom. St Theodosia, whose statue is in the Chapel of St Genevieve in St Sulpice (Paris) may be a third.

Isis in Black Virgin sites

About Isis at Le Puy (qv) much has already been said. Santa Sabina, mother house of the Dominican order, and the most perfect example of a Roman Christian basilica, had already in the fourth century, after the Council of Ephesus, been built over a Temple of Isis, near the temples of Juno and Diana. Also in Rome, the oldest Madonna in the world, the brown Virgin of the

4. Paris (Neuilly)

catacomb of Priscilla, is considered by some authorities to be Isis. In the cathedral of Metz (qv), the coronation church of the Lorraine dynasty where St Bernard preached the Crusade, a statue of Isis was also venerated as the Virgin until the sixteenth century. The effigy of the Graouly, a dragon drowned by St Clement in the Seille, can be seen in the crypt. The worship of Isis, introduced into Lucera (qv Italy) by sea-going Apulians, may have been one influence in the rise of the cult of the Black Virgin there.

The Black Virgin of Boulogne-sur-Mer illustrates the special relationship linking Isis to Merovingian France. In AD 633, during the reign of Dagobert I, king of all France, who may have been attending Sunday Mass there at the time, a ship sailed into the harbour, without oars or sails, containing nothing but a statue, three feet high, of the Black Virgin and a copy of the Gospels in Syriac. These last would almost certainly have been the version known as 'The Gospel of the Mixed', based on the Diatessaron of the second-century Gnostic, Tatian. In another legend, illustrated in a fifteenth-century church window, the boat is drawn by swans. The French *cygne* is homophonous with *signe*, 'a sign', which points us to the Swan Knight, Lohengrin or Helias, the son of Parzival, the Grail Knight, and the putative grandfather of Godefroy de Bouillon, who was born in Boulogne. St Ida, Godefroy's mother, built the old crypt of the cathedral, where there is a replica of Godefroy's tomb. From 1104, shortly after Godefroy's capture of Jerusalem and the foundation of the Latin Kingdom there under his brother, Baldwin, another Black Virgin began to be venerated at the church of Our Lady of the Holy Blood in Boulogne. Louis XI, perhaps recognising the precedence of an older line, but mainly motivated by shrewd political reasons of state, bestowed the suzerainty of the Boulonnais into the hands of Notre-Dame de Boulogne. (See also Valenciennes and Vichy.)

Who is the invisible helmsman of the barque of Isis? The Grand Master of the Prieuré de Sion has exactly this title, Nautonnier. In the *langue des oiseaux, bateau* is linked not only with *batelier,* boatman, but also with Le Bateleur, master of the Tarot, trickster, juggler and controller of the elements. By a stretch of the imagination it could yield us *le batisseur,* the builder or mason.

OTHER GODDESSES

Aphrodite/Venus

Venus was a rustic garden goddess with little cult in Rome until taken over by Aphrodite of Erice (cf. Custonaci) whose temple was built in the city in 217 BC. After that she became popular throughout the Empire. In her native land Aphrodite is sometimes represented as black, as a small votive statue of her in Cyprus, swathed in a star- or rose-covered robe proves. Geoffrey Grigson who reports this exhibit, speaks of the existence of an Aphrodite of Darkness in Egypt and Crete and of Black Aphrodites at Mantinea in Arcadia, in a cypress wood on the outskirts of Corinth and at Thespiai. The Christian Saints Melanie ('black') may derive from this Aphrodite Melainis, whom Grigson considers to be mixed with Isis. Probably it is through Isis that some of the cult and attributes of Venus have been assimilated by Christianity, since her sexuality was too explicit to be borrowed directly by carvers or painters of Black Virgins, though towards the end of the classical era she became increasingly identified with heavenly love. Durand-Lefèbvre writes of a Black Virgin that still existed before the Second World War at Sainte-Vinère in Bucharest, whose silver face, turned coal black, aroused the enthusiasm of the faithful. Valvanera (Spain) is the Valley of Venus, and there was a temple to her at Montserrat. It is a curious coincidence that Phryne, the most beautiful of Greek courtesans, the model for Praxiteles' statues of Aphrodite, should bear a name on account of her dark complexion which means 'toad', the animal symbol of the Merovingian dynasty, transformed by some love goddess into the fleur de lys. The main survivor of the Venus cult in Christianity is probably that of the Magdalen and allied saintly penitents.

Athene/Minerva

The name of the goddess was remembered by the followers of the goddess of wisdom in the Cathar castle of Minerve, where Simon de Montfort burned to death 180 parfaits in 1210. The little carving of an owl that brings good luck on the outside wall of the Church of Notre Dame of Dijon, home of the Black Virgin, Notre-Dame de Bon Espoir, may be another souvenir. In

Toulouse, the Church of La Daurade was built on the site of a temple of Pallas Athene, whose statue was consecrated as that of the new Christian Virgin. She also had an important temple in Marseilles. In the middle of the seventh century, St Eloi, Bishop of Tournai, who had been master of the mint in Marseilles, warned the faithful against invoking Athene before weaving flax into linen. (See Lucera, Italy, and Vichy.)

Bona Dea

Michel Bertrand sees the origins of the Black Virgin in the cult of this goddess, but it is not certain with which 'good goddess' she should be associated. In Rome her proper name was Fauna or Damia, and her nocturnal orgiastic ceremonies were restricted to women. She is closely related to Maia. The various Black Virgins called 'la Bonne Mère' may well derive from her, as would Sicilian St Agatha (good). Her place in the calendar (5 February) makes her part of the Candlemas cycle that replaced the Lupercalia over which Faunus, husband of Fauna and son of Picus, presided. Bertrand also identifies her with St Martha. Both Bona Dea and Maia had a cult at Marseilles. In Sicily Bona Dea was probably an epithet for Demeter.

Ceres/Demeter

Demeter, a corn-goddess and minder of children, is sometimes shown as black (cf. Bona Dea). (See Authezat, Bucharest, Lucera and Monte Vergine, Italy.)

Fortuna/Fors

First-born of Jupiter, she is linked through her name and attributes not only to the wheel of fate (cf. St Catherine) but also to ports and the forum (cf. Clermont-Ferrand and Lyons). Roman emperors always kept a golden statue of her where they slept (cf. also Cybele).

Juno/Hera

Hera ('Lady'), the goddess of marriage and childbirth, is sometimes shown as black. She is often shown as enthroned, carrying a pomegranate and a flower. (See Crotone, Ragusa.)

Vacuna

Along with Bellona, Vitula and Victoria, one of the goddesses chiefly associated with Mars, she is known to have been worshipped in Farfa (Italy).

Vesta/Hestia (Shining One)

Vesta derives from the Sankskrit root 'Vas', light, a word which, in Latin, means a vessel. She was a virgin fire goddess and every hearth had its own Vesta, which no doubt became blackened by smoke. In the few extant representations she is always shown as veiled. A statuette was found in the ruins of her Temple on a hill called Le Verrou (bolt) at Montpellier, where the Black Virgin, Nostra Dama des Taoulas, has many fiery connections (cf. also Couterne and Valenciennes). One of Vesta's close associates, Tellus Mater, Mother Earth, is shown on a Roman bas-relief with an ox and a sheep beneath her feet, and two children on her lap, flanked by one woman with a swan and another with a sea-monster. Vesta symbolizes ideal motherhood. The Vestal Virgins in Rome offer an example of pre-Christian chastity vows.

GODS

Apollo

The worship of the sun-god in Gaul is generally connected with that of Abellio/Belen. (See St Bertrand-de-Comminges.)

Hercules

Hercules has an important cult in Chipiona (qv Spain). As Hercules the wanderer he is of major interest in the cult of the Black Virgin through his courtship of Pyrene. His road, the Via Herculea, from Cadiz to Rome, leads through areas rich in Black Virgins (cf. especially Manosque). The Gallic Hercules is a very different figure from the Greco-Roman divine hero. (Cf. The Dagda/Sucellus, Chapter 3. See also Paris.)

Hermes/Mercury

Although in many of the sites connected with this god he is chiefly to be seen as a Gallo-Roman version of Wotan or Belen christianized as St Michael (cf. Le Puy), there are still many instances of place names deriving from Hermes or Mercury in near proximity to a Black Virgin. St Hermes shares a feast-day,

28 August, with St Augustine, learned doctor of the Church and former Gnostic.

Janus
Janus is one of the most important Roman gods. His two faces illustrate not only his role as deity of beginnings, looking to past and future, but his essential duality as the original bisexual chaos and the form which emerged from it. Diana/Jana and Saturn are especially associated with him. He may have been gallicized into Jean (John), one of the companions of the Black Virgin.

Jupiter
Jupiter, the father of the gods, is generally too public, official and heavenly to be much associated directly with the cult of the Black Virgin, but he does look down from his mountain sites onto a number of her shrines. (See Arpajon Great St Bernard, Valenciennes, Laurie, Monjou, Boëge and Vichy.)

Mars
Probably quite important under various names in the Black Virgin cult, he overlaps with other gods such as Wotan and Belen. Sts Maurice and Martin may well be among his successors. His animals are the wolf, the horse and the woodpecker, the bird held by the Child on the lap of Notre-Dame de Verdelais and possibly of the Black Virgin of Einsiedeln. In Italy he was a god of agriculture as well as war, and had as companions the cow-like Vacuna and Vitula. (See Boulogne and Valenciennes.)

Saturn
For the most part he is best approached in France through his Celtic and Teutonic equivalents, but the Merovingian holy place of Stenay is connected with him, and the Saturnalia began on 23 December, feast-day of St Dagobert, who was murdered near by.

CHAPTER 3
Natural religion: the Celtic and Teutonic sources

Dame Nature and Mother Earth; stones hurled from heaven or the volcanic depths or washed up on the shore with shapes that evoke the feminine; mountains that resemble the breasts of the goddess; springs, hot or cold, that flow as water of life from her womb; wells and caves that lead to the mysterious realm of birth and death; dark forests where the way is uncertain and wild things dwell; corn-fields and gardens, flocks and herds — these are the theophanies of the goddess. The classical world worshipped her at one remove from her origins as a statue in a man-made temple, often in a city. This separation of cult and nature grew deeper and wider in Christianity. The old nature gods like Pan became the new devils; nature herself became suspect and woman was repressed.

The Celtic world in its own way was just as civilized, if less urban, than the Roman. In it women retained many of their matriarchal rights and freedoms in relation to men, and the goddess was worshipped in her own natural forms in her own natural habitat. Again and again in the stories of the Black Virgins, a statue is found in a forest or a bush, or discovered when ploughing animals refuse to pass a certain spot. The statue is then taken to the parish church, only to return miraculously by night to her own place, where a chapel is then built in her honour. Almost invariably her cult is associated with natural phenomena, especially healing waters or striking geographical features such as extinct volcanoes, confluences and subterranean lines of force. The Romans had taken over and adapted many of the sacred sites of the Celtic world, which the Christians were later, in their turn, to sanctify, but the spirit of the place remains Celtic, and still whispers something of its origins through the cult associated with it.

The Romans renamed the Celtic and Teutonic gods after their own, and Christianity converted them into its saints and angels.

As a result, it is difficult to recapture the essence of the original deity. Furthermore, the divine names differ according to the various Celtic peoples who utter them, though the archetypal patterns, such as the triple goddess, remain constant. Since most of the Black Virgins are to be found in the land of the Gauls rather than Britain, or Ireland, it will often be simpler to use their names for the gods. Another complication is the influence of Teutonic cults, pre- and post-Roman, and the weight that should be accorded to them. The similarities between Celtic and Teutonic deities are, however, such as to make their cults often indistinguishable.

The Celtic influence on the development of the Black Virgin cult was further, though indirectly, reinforced by six centuries of missionary activity and fraternal visits by Irish monks in Western Europe. The first of these, St Columbanus (550-615), sojourned in the Syrian quarter of Orléans, with its cults to the Black Virgin, St Mary of Egypt and the Magdalen. The last, St Malachy of the prophecies, died in the arms of his friend and biographer, St Bernard, at Clairvaux in 1148. Among Irish links with the Merovingians, it should be noted that St Dagobert, their last king, spent his formative years in refuge in Ireland.

Few Celtic cult objects have been preserved from the pre-Roman period. The standing stones, whether arranged in elaborate temples as at Avebury and Stonehenge, or isolated menhirs and dolmens, were erected by earlier peoples, though the Celts held them in awe and no doubt used them for their religious ceremonies. A small number of sites believed to be those of pre-Roman Celtic temples have been discovered, but, more typically, worship took place in sacred places that were unenclosed. The Monster of Noves (qv) is a rare stone figure from the third century BC, phallic and devouring, in an area (see also Vacquières and Maillane) where there are a number of Black Virgins, including one associated with Hecate, goddess of death and rebirth. The original Black Virgins of Chartres and Longpont probably started life as Celtic fertility idols. It is not unlikely that many others may have either originated as pagan statuettes or have been inspired by them. In 1984 nearly two hundred small wooden statues were excavated from a pool in the sanctuary of Sequana, near the source of the Seine. In contrast to the Greeks and the Romans, the Celts considered rivers to be goddesses rather than sons of Okeanos and manifestations of Neptune. Not only river sources but also wells, lakes and springs were consequently honoured by images of the feminine, life-giving spirit, sometimes in the form of a single goddess and often in that of the triple Matres.

Of the many Black Virgins found in trees it is difficult to be sure whether the underlying influence is more likely to be Celtic, Teutonic or one deriving ultimately from the cult of Artemis/Diana. The symbolical value of the tree is hermaphroditic: it is the manifestation of the phallic power and firmness linking earth and heaven, but the life-force oracularly interpreting the divine will speaks with the voice of the goddess.

Although, in general, throughout their centuries of wandering, the Celts seem to have adapted to and assimilated the spirits of the places where they found themselves, there are a number of deities, specifically Celtic, which have connections in place or time with the cult of the Black Virgin. The Celts themselves committed none of their religious lore to writing during the pre-Christian period. Theirs was an oral culture, and wisdom was passed by word of mouth from generation to generation in the colleges of the bards and Druids. The texts on which most of our knowledge of Celtic religion and myth are based are either Roman or Christian, from a period not later than the eighth century. Neither Romans nor Christians were interested in the profundities of Celtic religion, and were content either to formulate it in their own terms or to comment on the more striking racial features: the independence of Celtic women, the drunkenness of Celtic men, the savagery and intrepidity of the warriors, male and female, and curious practices like the ritual copulation of the kings of Ulster with a mare. It is, however, generally agreed that the basis of Celtic religion was a belief in reincarnation. Tir nan Og, the land of eternal youth where warriors disport themselves, awaiting rebirth or eternally freed from its chains, has much in common with Wotan's Valhalla. The long years of Druidic initiation, the oral inculcation of bardic lore and the intricacies of the Ogham script, ensured that the religion was an esoteric one, preserved through the secret knowledge of a spiritual elite. When Ireland eventually embraced Christianity as it did, without the fertilising blood of martyrs, it was a Christianity based on the experiential know-

ledge of holy men and women, nuns, monks and Culdees that
kept the flame of the spirit burning in the west and re-
evangelized Europe. The Celtic Church long clung to the
customs and tonsure of St John and maintained the Greek
liturgical calendar over against that of Rome. In the peaceful
transition between the old faith and the new, most of the feasts
and divinities of Gaeldom were accommodated within the
Christian framework.

THE CELTIC DIVINITIES

The Dagda/Ogmios/Gallic Hercules/Sucellus/Dispater/Orcus
The second-century Greek philosopher, Lucian of Samosata,
commented on the strange image of Herakles current among the
Celts. He is an old man at the end of his life, balding, white-
haired, burnt by the sun, more like Charon than the classical
hero, but bearing the same accoutrements. He leads a considerable crowd by means of gold and amber cords linking their ears
to his tongue. Though he wears the lion-skin and wields the club
and bow, his power is evidently that of the word.

The oldest of the Celtic gods, father of all and lord of perfect
knowledge, was known to the Irish as the Dagda. His grotesque
appearance, garbed as a peasant, ugly, pot-bellied and coarse,
with a gargantuan appetite, probably marks him out as inherited
by the Celts from an earlier people. His son, Ogma Sun-Face or
Ogmias, god of literature and eloquence, was the inventor of
Ogham, the Celtic alphabet. The Dagda's club, so large that it
would have taken eight men to carry it, dealt death at one end,
and life at the other. His second most prized possession was a
magic cauldron that could never be emptied. It has much in
common with the magic cauldrons of Wotan and the black
goddess Cerridwen, though in their case the inspirational aspects
of the contents are emphasized, but it is, no doubt, one of the
early prototypes of the Holy Grail. Herakles is also associated
with a cauldron-shaped vessel which he borrowed from the sun
in order to make his voyage to the west. Bran the Blessed had a
cauldron which could restore the dead to life, but without the
power of speech, and it is probably this aspect of the vessel,

symbolizing both death and rebirth, that made it and its possessor so popular among the Celts.

The chief feast day associated with the Dagda, when he consumed a huge meal of porridge from a hole in the ground and mated with the Morrigan, a black mermaid goddess of water and the underworld, took place at Samain, 1 November. This is the season of witchcraft and the dead, Hallowe'en, All Saints and All Souls. The decline of the year, however, is also the time of the new wine, Martinmas fairs and sausage feasts, as hams are salted away for the long winter months. Pluto/Dispater is the god of riches as well as the underworld and, in astrology, rules Scorpio (24 October-22 November). In Gaul he is known as Sucellus, and is represented as a mature figure with a massive mallet, proffering a large drinking cup. All Gauls claimed to be descended from him. Some representations of St James the Greater are evocative of Sucellus.

At the feast of Samain, which was the Celtic New Year, when one looked both forward and back on a day which belonged to neither year, the boundaries between the world of the living and that of the gods and the dead were blurred. Similarly, in Christian times, those who have died in the parish during the year walk in procession to the graveyard on All Soul's Day, before returning to the earth.

Symbolically, at this end and beginning of the year, the lord of the dead and the dark goddess unite to ensure that the earth will once more be fruitful after the dead season, when they will reemerge as the new light and blessed greenness of early February. The Church's calendar for the period of Samain includes, as well as All Saints and All Souls, the following feasts: Christ the King, the Holy Relics, St Hubert (the wild huntsman of the Ardennes), the black St Martin de Porres, St Malachy of Armagh, St Flour and a number of others with Merovingian, Teutonic and Black Virgin associations.

Lug

One of the four major feasts of the Celtic year was Lughnasad, Lammas, held on 1 August to commemorate the death of Lug. The fact that to the Anglo-Saxons it was 'loaf-mass' suggests that Lug represented, as the first fruits of the grain harvest, the sun as it enters upon its annual decline. His many-sidedness

precludes any possibility of seeing in him nothing but the dying
and rising god of a vegetation cult. He gives as his chief
occupation that of carpenter, which links him to Joseph, Jesus,
builders of arks and chariots, and all constructors of frameworks.
That he is armed with a magic spear, sired a hero, practised
sorcery, poetry, horsemanship and the blacksmith's craft, as well
as having a raven as his familiar, points to a strong association
with Wotan. His consort in the ancient capital and Black Virgin
site of Lyons, which takes its name from him, is called Rosmerta,
who at Sion-Vaudémont (qv) is Wotan's queen (see also St
Bertrand de Comminges). Lug's sling and his harp remind us of
King David. The lion, too, belongs to both of them as it does to
Cybele, the Lady of Lyons. The Greek root of his name, *luk*
wolf, links him to Apollo, Arcadian Zeus and the tribe of
Benjamin, but also has connotations with dawn and dusk, and
the path of light, the sun's annual course. The Latin words which
may be connected with him are *lux*, light, and *lucus*, a sacred
grove. He is also, like his homophone St Luke, a historian.
Robert Graves suggests both an identification with the three-fold
Geryon and a possible derivation from the Sumerian word for
'son'. Irish mythology makes him the offspring of the triple
goddess, a point well taken by the Church, which celebrates on 1
August the feast of Sts Faith, Hope and Charity, daughters of St
Wisdom. Lug's other major city in France, Laon, the Carolingian
capital, boasts a Black Virgin, a Templar Commandery and a
bull-festooned cathedral. There is a Luc-sur-Aude between
Rennes-le-Château and Limoux (qv) and a Luc-sur-Mer next to
La Délivrande (qv). The comparative rarity of the name in
France has led some to believe it was the unnameable name of
God.

Bell/Belen/Belenus

Belen is another Celtic god of light, important for the study of
the cult of the Black Virgin. Beaune is named for him or his
latinized consort Bellona, later assimilated with Cybele. An
image of him was found at Beaune in 1767 and her likeness
appeared on the ancient arms of the city. Mont St Michel, where
the Black Virgin was once known as Notre-Dame du Mont
Tombe, was originally Tombelen. Nearby was a temple o
Cybele. Bollène and Ballon no doubt owe their names to the god

as do the many villages called St Bonnet to be found near Black Virgin sites. It seems improbable that the 28th Bishop of Clermont, who died in Lyons in 710, and whose body was brought home sewn up in the skin of a billy-goat, could have inspired such a large number of Church dedications if there were not some other motivation at work. The St Bonnet three kilometres from Riom had a temple to Belen, while at St Bonnet near St Germain l'Herm, where there was a temple of Diana, a phallic stone surmounted by a cross still survives. St Bonnet shares a feast-day, 15 January, with St Maurus (Mars). Belen, the Gallic Apollo, or Abellio, may also be the inspiration for Notre-Dame des Abeilles, the Black Virgin of Banyuls.

Belen seems to have been a more erotic god than Apollo. His feast is May Day with its Beltane fires when the licentious rites of the maypole were performed in honour of Flora/Maia/Venus, the May Queen. According to Saillens, Mont Saint Michel may have been in pagan times a resort of sacred prostitutes where the rites of Bacchus and Venus were celebrated at all seasons. 1 May, now the feast of St Joseph the Workman, was once that of St Amador in his own shrine of Rocamadour, where the Black Virgin succeeded to Sulevia, Minerva, Iduenna, a triple goddess integrated by Cybele. The eve of May Day sees the feasts of St Catherine of Siena, the bride of Christ, and one of a number of saints called Sophia. Belen's daughter, Arianrhod, who as lady of the silver celestial wheel (the Corona Borealis) is related to that other Catherine, of Alexandria, became the bride of Gwydion, considered by Robert Graves to be a Welsh form of Wotan. A daughter of the Greek Belos, ancestor of the Danaans, whom some associate with the Tuatha de Danaan in Ireland, was the bi-sexual, child-stealing Lamia.

Cernunnos

If Lug and Bel are translatable more or less interchangeably into the Gallic Mercury and Apollo, Cernunnos is less easily assimilated to classical modes. Robert Graves associates him with Actaeon. Joseph Campbell equates him with the Dagda. He is represented as the central god of a trinity, flanked by Mercury and Apollo, naked, effeminate youths in comparison with the powerful, mature, horned figure, seated cross-legged on a throne, beneath which a stag and a bull feed on the plenteous fodder which flows from his lap. On the Gundestrup Bowl, where he assumes the semi-lotus yoga position, he is surrounded by animals and holds a ram-headed serpent in his left hand. A figure riding a large fish is swimming away from him. A stele from Beaune museum shows him as the three-headed central figure of a triad of naked seated gods. Another carving found under Notre-Dame de Paris in 1911 shows the god with rings on his horns, glancing fixedly sideways. He almost certainly stems from the shamans to be seen weaving their hunting spells in prehistoric cave-paintings. Emma Jung and M.-L. von Franz relate him to Wotan and Merlin as well as to Christ, who in the Grail legends appeared to his disciples as a white stag. He lingers on in Christian hagiography as St Hubert, patron of hunters, and St Eustace whose emblem is also the stag. In England he may be remembered as Herne the Hunter, who had a great oak at Windsor, in the Abbots Bromley horn dance and as the Cerne Giant. In Scotland he is shown on a stone-carving as a merman with two tails.

Horned gods are by definition cuckold gods. Franck Marie suggests the hypothesis that the cuckolded god is one belonging to an earlier age. If Belen belongs to the age of Aries which ended with the coming of the Piscean saviour, Christ, Cernunnos harks back to the Taurean era of the great goddesses. Marie sees Cernunnos as the eremitic spirit of Mt Bugarach, the sacred Cathar mountain, halfway from Montségur to the sea. A stream called La Blanque flows from Bugarach to be joined by the Fontaine des Amours and another, variously called La Gode (a title of Freyja/Frigg/Hel) or La Madeleine which rises on Mt Serbairou. The confluence of these streams with the Sals takes place at Rennes-les-Bains, and all journey on together to the Aude, passing the Black Virgin of Limoux.

The Abbé Boudet of Rennes-les-Bains, mentor of the Abbé Saunière of Rennes-le-Château, wrote a strange book, published in 1886, *La Vraie Langue Celtique et le cromlech de Rennes-les-Bains* which was apparently much appreciated by Queen Victoria. Amidst a farrago of humorously false etymology and questionable history, he asserts that the Celtic inhabitants of the area (including Toulouse), the Volscian Tectosages, were the ancestors of the Franks and the sons of Gomer. Gomer was the son of Japhet, who came from Ceylon and India to the west via

Troy. Through him the Merovingians can thus claim to be descended from Noah. There are indeed some surprising place names in the area, like Goundhill, with its curious echoes of Goonhilly in the far west of Cornwall (one French euphemism for to be a cuckold is 'to go to Cornwall'), an odd neighbour for such Balkan-sounding peaks as Bugarach and Serbairou.

Perhaps some of the esoteric teaching associated with Cernunnos persisted in the Christian era. Marie hints at a mystery surrounding the nick-name 'Coucoupierre' given to Peter the Hermit, preacher and leader of the First Crusade. He was reputedly one of the Calabrian solitaries who settled in the Black Lands of the Golden Valley (see Orval, Belgium) where he became the tutor of Godefroy de Bouillon. The Latin *cuculus*, a cuckoo or adulterer, is very close to *cucullus*, a cowl, a similarity which no doubt accounts for the unusual cognomen of the monk. Did he perhaps introduce some teachings from the past that were not wholly orthodox into his woodland classes in the Ardennes? Joachim of Flora (1132-1202), who taught the imminent coming of the age of the Holy Spirit, a notion which was condemned by the Church, was from the same syncretistic southern Italian tradition as Peter the Hermit and experienced a conversion to the interior life in the Holy Land before becoming a Cistercian. He is named for St Joachim, who with his wife, St Anne, must be the most pre-Christian of saints. He shares his feast-day, 16 August, the day after the Assumption, with St Roch (qv), the companion of Black Virgins. St Anne's day is 26 July. On the 25th the memory is venerated of St Christopher, a Canaanite giant who carried the world on his shoulders in the form of the infant Christ, and affords Templar-like protection to pilgrims and wayfarers. The same day is the feast of St James the Greater of Compostela and of the curiously named St Cucufas. ('it is right to be cuckoo'?), also known as Quiquenfat, Guinefort and Cugat, called a Prince of Scotland in his chapel at Le Puy.

Teutates, Esus and Taranis

Lucan (AD 39-65) of Cordoba, nephew of Seneca, whose Stoic views he shared, writes of this trinity of Celtic gods in his *Pharsalia*: 'Mercury, among the Gauls, is called Teutates and is propitiated by immersing the victim head first in a cauldron of water until he is drowned; to satisfy Mars, called Esus, they hang

the victim on a tree and quarter him. For Taranis they offer
burnt sacrifice in a wickerwork idol, filled with men.'

Marie traces modified survivals of such cults up to modern
times in the traditions of carnival at Limoux (qv). The similarity
of the name Esus, the woodman god, associated with hanging on
a tree, to that of the crucified carpenter, Jesus, may have
furthered an ease of transition between the two religions. A first-
century AD bas-relief shows Esus cutting down a willow-tree
containing a bull's head and three marsh birds, a scene
comparable to that of the hero Gilgamesh cutting down the tree,
also probably a willow, of the goddess Ishtar. Christians
enthusiastically felled the sacred trees of Germany, but already
the trees of the Taurean divinities had been hewn down by the
votaries of the age of Aries. Julius Caesar had personally axed an
ancient sacred grove at Marseilles, because all others feared the
retribution of the goddess (cf. Chapter 2, Artemis — the coin of
Myrrha). It thus seems possible that the placing of images of a
goddess in a tree may be a cultic practice, dating back to the age
of Taurus, which has survived to this day in numerous traditions
relating to the Black Virgin. The Black Virgin of Neuerburg (qv
Germany) was not removed from her tree until April 1984. It
would seem that, like Zeus at Dodona, the gods of the Celts and
Teutons may have taken over trees sacred to an older goddess
without totally banishing her presence.

The Matres

Triads of gods are, as we have seen, an important feature in
Celtic and Teutonic religion. There are, in addition, representations of three-headed deities, bulls with three horns, boars with
three tusks, a bull with three cranes, the three sacred birds that
guard the Isle of Man, etc., but the most widespread devotion
among the Celts seems to have been the cult of the triple-
goddess. Like triple Hecate, she rules over the three realms of
sky, earth and underworld, presiding over birth, life and death.
Wells and springs are the openings of her womb, and her moon
governs the growth, flow and decay of all that is on earth. The
triads are shown in different forms and venerated under a variety
of names, as maiden, bride and crone. Typically they carry horns
of plenty. Their distribution is wider than that of the male gods
and they appear to date from an earlier period, being par-

ticularly popular among the poorer sections of the population, always more resistant to cultic novelties.

Rosmerta

This goddess is usually considered to be the consort of the Gallic Mercury and has been represented carrying the caduceus herself. Her cult was particularly prevalent in eastern Gaul, though images of her have been found as far west as Gloucestershire. At Sion-Vaudémont (qv), where she is the consort of the universal god Wotan, an *ex-voto* plaque erected by Carinius, thanking her and Mercury/Wotan for the safety of his son, Urbicus, was discovered in 1817. There is also a statue of her in Sion museum. At Lyons she was accounted the companion of Lug. She has been seen as a personification of fruitful mother earth, but her form and her name could also be suggestive of Venus, as could the sexual cult of the Virgin and the Holy Spirit which flourished at Sion in the mid-nineteenth century. To judge by her chief location in old Lotharingia, Rosmerta partakes, as an intermediate figure, of both the Celtic and Teutonic worlds. The Gaelic *ros* means either 'wood', or 'prominence', 'peninsula', 'headland', while the Germanic *hros* signifies horse. The Latin roots yield 'rose' and 'dew'. Merta is a puzzle. Most other *mart*-words find their ultimate origin in Mars, like Wotan, the god of War, or Martha, 'lady'. The Sanskrit root *mrt* means dead. The myrtle, on the other hand, sacred to Aphrodite/Venus, is a symbol of the feminine principle, associated with happiness, victory and initiation into the divine mysteries. The Greek *murtos* means both myrtle and clitoris. At the end of the last century a beautiful androgynous statue was excavated at Sion, reminding us that Venus carrying a caduceus might well be considered as Hermaphrodite, and that Gnostic sexual rites, of which those carried out at Sion were a late echo, were designed to restore the primal androgyny. In this borderland of Teuton and Celt one may also suspect the influence of Nerthus, androgynous mother, by her brother, of the love-goddess Freyja. According to de Sède, who sees her as the origin of the Black Virgin of Avioth, Rosmerta was attended by a cortège of dead children (p.23).

Epona/Rhiannon/Macha

Epona enjoyed a more widespread devotion than any other Celtic goddess, having been adopted as the patroness of Roman cavalry stables and carried by the legions to all parts of the Empire. She is shown riding side-saddle wearing a diadem and a long robe with a curious swirling, circular, four-fold halo or banneret of material billowing behind her head. She carries a key, a symbol also associated with Hecate, and gazes fixedly in front of her. This bas-relief was found at Gannat, a dozen miles from the initiates' church of Thuret (qv) where there is in addition to the famous Black Virgin, a remarkable font around which a uroboric horse bites its own tail. Sometimes Epona's horse or mare is accompanied by a foal (cf. stele in Beaune Museum). The Kings of Ulster used to mate ritually with a mare and the Queens of India with a stallion.

Horses, symbols of libido and death, are associated with a number of Black Virgin sites: Einsiedeln is the oldest and most

5. Thuret

famous centre of horse-breeding in Switzerland and the stud-
farms of Saumur and those near Sion-Vaudémont are well-
known in France. In England, Lady Godiva and the White Horse
of Uffington testify to the durability of the goddess, though it
should be remembered that the horse is sacred to Wotan and
Freyja too. Perhaps the white horse of Belgic Kent, invaded by
Hengist and Horsa ('stallion' and 'horse'), belongs to both Celt
and Teuton. In Christian iconography, the horse is associated
with St George, a Christianized figure from pagan myth, recently
demoted by the Church. He doubtless owes his rulership of
England to his resemblance to Wotan. St James also appears on a
white charger at Compostela to rout the Moors. In Ireland,
Macha and Mabd are equivalent to Epona as protectors of
horses and chthonic divinities. The Welsh mare-goddess
Rhiannon was queen of Dyfed, whose central point was the
'Dark Gate', entrance to the underworld.

Brigit/Anu/Danu/Dana

According to the *Larousse Encyclopedia of Mythology* it seems
probable that all these deities are different concepts of the same
mother-goddess figure. In Saillens's view the Black Virgin of
Tarascon (qv), one of whose titles is 'La Belle Briançonne' is a
combination of Brigit and Ana/Anu. Brigantia was the eponymous goddess of the powerful tribe of the Brigantes, the most
populous in Britain, whose capital was York. Further south her
name extends from Briançon (the Gallo-Roman Brigantium) in
the Alps to Brigantia (now Corunna) in the far north-west
corner of Spain. The neighbours of the Brigantes in Yorkshire
were the Parisii, founders of Paris, evidence of the Celtic capacity
for wandering.

Brigit is especially associated with the cult of the Black Virgin
through the feast Imbolc, one of the Celtic quarter days, which
occurred on 1 February, now the feast of St Brigid, the Mary of
the Gael, which coincides with Candlemas. Like Candlemas it
was the celebration of the reawakening of the secret fire that
would purify the land and herald the return of spring. The trial
marriages that took place on that day, which lasted by mutual
consent for a year, illustrate the comparative freedom of Celtic
women to decide their own fate. At Beltane, on 1 May, Brigit,
representing the Tuatha de Danaan, the people of the goddess

Danu, with whom she is probably identified, married Bres, who was half African, a giant Fomorian descended from Noah's son Ham, whose people were the earlier inhabitants of Ireland. Brigit (Irish 'Brig' = 'power') was a goddess of poetry, knowledge and the arts of civilization. Her shrine of the sacred fire at Kildare was continued by her Christian namesake, St Brigid or Bride (c.450–c.523). Bridewell, the chief women's prison in London, was once a convent of hers. Other features which St Brigid shares with many Black Virgins are her ability to raise the dead and the healing power of the cloth that has touched her, especially when applied to women suffering from barrenness and illnesses of childbirth.

St Bridgit, patron saint of Sweden, shares her feast day, 8 October, with three penitent whores, Margaret, Pelagia and Thais, as well as with St Bacchus. In 1346 she founded an order devoted to learning, the Brigittines, whose members were organized in double communities of men and women, like Cassian's foundation in Marseilles and St Brigid's at Kildare. In the new order, however, the prioress was the superior of both houses. Syon House was their headquarters in England. According to Robert Graves, some houses of the order 'reverted merrily to paganism'. The dark-faced St Mary of Egypt is associated by Graves with the Brigid/Bridgit archetype.

The syllable most commonly found in the names of goddesses throughout Europe and the Middle East is *an*. The Indo-Germanic root signifies 'to breathe', from which are derived *anemos* (wind), *animus* (spirit) and *anima* (soul). The Hebrew 'Hannah', name of the mothers of Samuel and the Virgin Mary, means, like John, 'God has favoured'. In Greek *ana* means 'O King', a form restricted to invocation of the gods, though Sappho is said to have used it as the vocative of *anassa*, meaning 'queen, lady or mistress' as applied to goddesses. *An* in Sumerian means 'heaven' while the Latin for a duck is *anas*. In general, throughout the Indo-European languages, the most prevalent associations with *ana* have to do with plenty and motherhood. This aspect of her is illustrated by the twin hills called the Paps of Anu in County Kerry. The Aryan conquerors of the Himalayas consecrated one of its great peaks to Anna Purna.

But the goddess also had a dark, devouring side, well illustrated in the legend of Black Annis or Cat Anna of Leicester, who lived in a cave she had clawed out for herself in the Dane (Danu?) Hills. She used to lie in wait for children by a huge pollard oak where she would hang their skins to dry after clawing them to death, sucking their blood and flaying them. She had a secret passage in later times leading from her lair to the cellars under the castle, and as late as 1941 a small girl evacuated from the city reported that you could hear her grinding her teeth five miles away. Black Annis may seem a far cry from the Christian goddess until one recalls that the speciality of Black Virgins is to grant eternal bliss to dead babies offered to them (cf. Avioth). This death aspect is also illustrated by the Irish great goddess, the Morrigan, especially associated with war and destruction, who hovers near the battle-field as a crow or raven.

The Roman goddess Anna Perenna was considered to be the sister of Belus the father of Danaus and Lamia, though Beli (Belen) was also said to be the son of Anna, 'Empress of Rome'. It is as St Anne that this potent symbol persists in Christianity. To the Bretons, according to Saillens, she largely replaces the Black Virgin (but see Guingamp). Her window in Chartres, the biggest image in the Cathedral, has been black since its donation by St Louis in the thirteenth century. Jean Markale talks of the submerged princess of Breton legends, the ruler of hell, who has dared to resist authority, and so is necessarily 'a bad and lewd woman'. Like Hecate, she rules the cross-roads by night and, like Lilith, she is the Devil's consort. Markale goes on, 'Yet surely she is the reflection of the goddess of ancient, pre-patriarchal societies . . . who haunts every corner of life, but reveals herself only very reluctantly, sometimes even as a Black Virgin.'

The Loathly Damsel

Perhaps it is this submerged princess who, at the very end of the Celtic era, seeks to bring about the redemption of an imprisoned maiden from the stately castle on a lofty mountain. According to the Mabinogion, a maiden came to King Arthur's court at Caerleon to reproach Peredur/Pereceval for not having asked about the streaming spear in the Castle of Wonders (the Grail Castle) where there is also a bleeding head. She rode a yellow mule and 'blacker were her face and her two hands than the blackest iron covered with pitch'.

THE TEUTONIC DEITIES

The possible influence of the Germanic tradition on the cult of the Black Virgin has received little attention. Yet the vast majority of Black Virgins are to be found in those areas of Europe which, at the break-up of the Roman Empire, came under the domination of the Arian Burgundians and Visigoths. Certain factors made a transition from paganism to the heretical Christianity of Arius easier than the acceptance of orthodox Catholicism.

The gods of the Germans were not far removed from the world of men. They were viewed as ancestors, heroes and kings of old, in whom shone the light of the absolute, and who still, like Wotan, rode the night-skies on wind-fast steeds or wandered in the forests of middle earth befriending those in need. The idea that Jesus Christ could have been consubstantial with the absolute godhead and begotten by him before all worlds would have been thoroughly alien to Teutons who claimed descent from, and kinship with, their own high god. Arianism, on the other hand, denying as it did, the full divinity of Christ, was welcomed by the Goths and Burgundians. Much in the gospel would, in fact, have been quite familiar to them. The rune for Wotan, strongly resembling a crucified man, recalls the similarity of his sacrifice, hanging nine days on a tree to bring saving knowledge to mankind, with that of Jesus (known to the Goths as Frauja). Wotan, too, received his initiation into the waters of wisdom through the mediation of a relation of his mother's, Mimir, who, later, like John the Baptist, lost his head.

Wotan embalmed the head of Mimir, and cast spells upon it so that it could continue to tell him of hidden things. Wotan also brought the speaking head of Minos, Lord of the Underworld, to Scandinavia. In later history, speaking heads were associated with Gerbert of Aurillac, Roger Bacon, the Portuguese giant Ferragus, and St Albertus Magnus, Dominican alchemist whose tomb is in the Black Virgin city of Cologne. The 'wonderful head' of the god Bran, buried under the Tower of London until excavated by King Arthur, together with the ravens that are the tutelary spirits of London, offer further parallels to the Wotan cult. Darcy and Angebert associate a triple head from Bornholm, sacred island of the Burgundians, with a wotanic ritual, and point to a possible continuity between it and the head Baphomet used in Templar initiation ceremonies. The Baphomet carved by the Templars awaiting death at Chinon assumes, according to Yvon Roy, different faces when looked at from different angles and in varying lights. One possible example of a Baphomet may be found on a capital of the Templar church of Eunate (Spain), where a prophet, inverted, becomes a goat. Unquestionably the most dynamic and tenacious successors to the Templars were the Teutonic Knights, a highly wotanic order and faithful servants of the black eagle, whether with one head or two.

Wotan/Odin/Woden

Wotan offers a unique example of a European god in opposition to Christianity who, far from being a spent force, was beginning to reach his apogee during the first millennium of our era, being cut off in his prime and thoroughly repressed by the terrorist tactics of Charlemagne. If the cult of the Black Virgin attracts to itself elements from other, submerged, cults, it would be surprising if Wotan, the master of disguise and infiltration, were not represented in it. Indeed, his involvement with the ambiguous traditions of Sion-Vaudémont (qv) are undeniable. It seems likely that Einsiedeln (qv), with its dragon fountain, in the heart of old Switzerland, where Wotan still rides the sky with his retinue of souls, 'the holy people', preserves memories of the usurped god. The ancient *dalle du cavalier* at Rennes-le-Château is believed to represent the young King Sigebert IV and his knight Mérovée Lévi. May it not be that these two figures, Templar-like on one horse, stem from an iconographic tradition celebrating Wotan the saviour's rescue of his protégé, Hadding, from the hands of his foes?

The Romans identified Wotan with Mercury/Hermes. Both are tricksters and guides of souls who are often depicted wearing a broad-brimmed hat. With St Joseph they share the same day of the week, Wednesday (though in Germany the neutral Mittwoch has been tactfully substituted) and all three bestow a fortunate death. This, however, is only a small part of the repertoire of a god who was well on his way to attaining universality through assimilation of the attributes of his competitors, much as Isis was doing at the same period. His similarities with the war-god Mars/Ares are particularly strong. His name means 'rage'

('Wotan, id est furor', Adam of Bremen, eleventh-century archbishop), he is bearded, carries a spear and wears a helmet. As lord of hosts he throws into battle his irresistible, frenzied shock-troops, the Berserkers. Like Jupiter/Zeus, whose eagle he shares, he is the all-father, notorious for his amorous escapades, presiding jovially over a table of good cheer.

A raven-god like Saturn/Kronos, Wotan's great feast is Saturnalia or Yuletide, twelve nights at least which, disguised as St Nicholas, he has wrested back from the encroachments of Christianity, replacing the cross with his world-tree. *Larousse* compares Wotan as a sky-god to Varuna and Uranus. It is curious that Uranus, who has very little mythology, is increasingly seen by astrologers (as he was by Gustav Holst) as the magician, whose sudden strokes of fate turn everything upside down in revolutionary fashion. Such is Wotan, who raises up his favourites, only to cast them down at the height of their glory. If Wotan is assimilating Uranus, the ruler of the coming age of Aquarius, then it is important that the world should recognize Wotan's depth and wisdom. The Wotanic frenzy is essentially that of the shaman and seer rather than the warrior with which he is generally associated. He is a wine-god, like Jesus and Dionysus, and takes no other nourishment than the fermented juice of the grape. Wotan brought wisdom and Gnosis from the underworld and is, like Pluto, the lord of the dead.

In his chthonic role he is no doubt succeeded by Blaise, consort of the Black Virgin of Candlemas, whose name in Celtic means 'wolf', the animal most closely associated with Wotan. The crossed candles of Blaise applied to the throat remove blockages and assist communication, but they also resemble the cross of St Andrew, the saltire of Scotland and Burgundy. This symbol is the Teutonic rune of the eagle.

As lord of Minne (love) he vies with Eros and Christ and, perhaps, since he can change his sex, with Venus herself, Freyja. It is this repressed aspect of Wotan that especially relates him to much in the cult of the Black Virgin. His beloved Brünnhilde, whose disobedience ushered in the new age of humanity, had a daughter, the last of the Volsungs, Aslog. She lived on in Norway as a sooty-faced kitchen-maid whose name means 'raven'. Another female raven, according to Marion Bradley, was a priestess of Avalon, founded by Wotan's British counterpart, Merlin.

Frigg

Frigg is Wotan's second wife (the first being Jord/Erde), the goddess for whom Friday is named, identified by the Romans with Venus, but more strongly associated with marriage and child-bearing, and invoked by women in labour. Friday used to be considered a lucky day for weddings in Germany. Frigg was a powerful intercessor who prevailed upon Wotan to spare the Lombards to whom he had decreed defeat at the hands of the Vandals. She also persuaded Wotan to grant the request of King Rerir and his wife for a child. In these ways she fulfils functions very characteristic of the Black Virgins. Perhaps she is associated with Rosmerta, who at Sion, combines features of the mother, lover and bringer of victory.

Freyja

Freyja and Frigg are often confused and sometimes indistinguishable, but Freyja possesses a number of important individual traits. Snorri, writing in c. 1220, calls her the most renowned of the goddesses and the only one still alive i.e. still the object of cultic veneration. If Frigg is Hera, protectress of married love, Freyja is Venus, goddess of love affairs and, in her own mythical tradition, the northern representative of the whore, wisdom. Her wisdom, like that of Loki and Wotan, is shamanistic: assuming the form of a bird, she can fly through the nine worlds bringing back knowledge and power to her petitioners. Thus she became identified by Christians with the queen of the night and of witches, and as such she is represented, like Diana, naked, her cloak flying behind her as she rides her broomstick through the air, on a twelfth-century wall-painting in Schleswig cathedral. As Gertrude ('spear-strength'), one of the Valkyries who were once her priestesses, she shares a feast-day, 17 March, with a number of interesting saints. These include St Gertrude of Nivelles, a city reputedly named after the Niebelungen, situated between the Black Virgin sites of Hal and Walcourt, where giants and a magical horse called Godet are still celebrated at carnival time. It is also the feast of St Joseph of

Arimathea, who brought the Holy Grail to Glastonbury. One pilgrim to Glastonbury was that man of many voyages, St Patrick, who has made 17 March famous wherever the Irish have travelled.

Freyja has much to do with horses, and may well be the original nightmare. Her devotees could assume the form of horses and were also accused of riding men to death on their beds. As a flax-goddess, Freyja is clearly related to the Slav Serpolnica, who also rapes men to death. One of Freyja's names, Mardoll, suggests a connection with the sea and may link her with Nehalennia, the goddess of Walcheren in the Scheldt estuary. This was the homeland of the Franks, where Mérovée/Merweg was engendered. Nehalennia is sometimes represented standing in the stern of a boat, like Isis and the Black Madonna who sailed in Merovingian times into the harbour of Boulogne. Boulogne is a great deal closer to Middelburg than to Alexandria, the home port of that other, more celebrated ship-goddess, Isis, star of the sea. Nehalennia is also represented, like St Roch and Hecate, with a dog, which may relate her to Freyja in her aspect as goddess of the dead. Freyja's other feast-day, 2 February, coincides with Candlemas, St Brigid's Imbolc festival, and day *par excellence* of the Black Virgin. Freyja's car is drawn by swans and doves.

Hel

Hel/Hella refers both to the place of the dead and to the goddess who presides there though, like Hecate, she has power, granted by Wotan, in all the worlds. Her head hung forward, partially disguising the fact that she possessed only half a face (cf. Champagnac-lec-Mines). The Belgian Black Virgin city of Hal (qv) has also been etymologically connected with Hel.

CHAPTER 4
The whore wisdom in the Christian era

There is nothing in the New Testament that offers much justification for a cult of the feminine principle as divine wisdom, mother of God or queen of heaven. Mary's role is dealt with in a few lines, and, after the narrative of the nativity, seems sometimes at odds with her son's mission. So how is it that little more than a century after the conversion of Constantine, the triumph of Mary Theotokos, the God-bearer, was celebrated on the altars of Christendom from the Rhône to the Euphrates?

There are two main reasons for this phenomenon. One, the great expansion during the later Roman Empire of the religion of universal goddesses such as Isis and Cybele, was discussed in Chapter 2. The other is more complex, and concerns the effect on Christianity of its first three centuries of struggle against Gnosticism, its hydra-headed adversary.

By the beginning of the Christian era, a fusing and blending of traditions had already been in progress for some centuries in the great mixing bowl of Alexandria. The vast Jewish population, worshipping one masculine, invisible God, and abhorring graven images, was surrounded on every hand by the deities and philosophies of Greece and Egypt. The translation of the Hebrew Bible into Greek in the third century BC had a subtle but profound effect on the way Jews came to think about God and the world. One of their greatest writers, Philo of Alexandria (*c*.20 BC–AD50) contributed to the development of a symbolic understanding of scripture that was later to be the hallmark of the Christian catechetical school led by Clement of Alexandria (*c*.150–*c*.215). Philo coined a word, 'archetype', to denote an exemplar, pattern or model, literally 'first-moulded', to refer to certain principal ideas, not far removed from those of Plato. They were not quite the same as the pagan gods of popular religion, but neither were they mere abstractions or dead concepts. A good example of such an archetype is 'the Word' used in the prologue to St John's Gospel to mean an intermediary power between God and the world. In the period separating Philo from Clement, Christianity in Egypt was dominated by the Gnostic tendency, which emphasized the importance of such influences emanating from the godhead. Many of these semi-personified abstract nouns, which demand to be capitalized, are feminine: Wisdom, Silence, Truth, Thought, Faith, Grace, Life, Church and Gnosis itself — intuitive, experiential knowledge or insight.

The Gnostics thus counterbalanced a slide, in both Judaism and Christianity, away from the feminine. St John's 'Word', for example, the unambiguously masculine 'Logos', borrows its attributes from the feminine 'Wisdom' who was with God before the creation. Similarly, 'Spirit', neuter in Greek and masculine in Latin, is, in its original Hebrew form, feminine, a fact which the Gnostics never forgot. Furthermore it was not just feminine words which played an important part in Gnosticism; women were leaders and teachers in their groups and could even act as deacon, priest or bishop if it fell to their lot. No doubt this is the reason St Paul, or someone using his name, forbade women to speak in church.

To the Gnostic, the importance of objective phenomena lies in their underlying symbolic significance, and the preoccupation of the later Church with concrete, literal, historic facts is quite alien to them. As a result, it is often difficult to be sure whether they are talking about real people or archetypal forces. Thus, Simon Magus, a contemporary of Christ's and an early Gnostic teacher, known to the Church as father of all heresies, was also acknowledged by his followers as the Great Power of God. His chief companion was Helen, whom he rescued from a brothel in Tyre and who is also Ennoia, the First Thought of God, Divine Wisdom, who fell into matter, suffering ever greater degradation with each incarnation, until the Great Power redeemed her. Similar claims are, of course, made concerning Christ, who came to redeem the lost sheep of the house of Israel, and whose biography is hardly less shadowy. Concerned as they were with the sufferings of fallen Sophia, Gnostics discerned a pattern in the relationship between Jesus and Mary Magdalene similar to that between Simon and Helen. Here is how the Magdalen is described in the Gnostic Gospel of Philip:

As for the Wisdom who is called 'the barren', she is the mother of the angels. And the companion of the Saviour is Mary Magdalene. But Christ loved her more than all the disciples and used to kiss her often on the mouth. The rest of the disciples were offended by it and expressed disapproval. They said to him, 'Why do you love her more than all of us?' The Saviour answered and said to them, 'Why do I not love you like her? When a blind man and one who sees are both together in darkness, they are no different from one another. When the light comes then he who sees will see the light, and he who is blind will remain in darkness'. . . . His sister and his mother and his companion were each a Mary.

The Gospel of Philip also reveals that 'It is by a kiss that the perfect conceive and give birth.' In the Gospel of Mary she is represented as being in communication with the risen Lord, endowed with knowledge, vision and insight far exceeding Peter's and the other disciples'. In 'The Dialogue of the Saviour' she is described, in terms worthy of Isis, as the 'woman who knew the All'.

The dictionary definition of 'magdalen' is 'reformed prostitute' and Sophia is called 'Prunikos' (= lewd). One of the titles of Aphrodite, who is also Queen of Heaven, is 'Porné', the whore. Why should wisdom be portrayed as a whore? Perhaps because she is there for all who want her, crying on the roof-tops and displaying her wares for those who can afford them. Wisdom is, then, accessible, but in a despised and unexpected guise. To Gnostics and Christians alike what tended to be disregarded was the world of matter. Catholics saw it as the good creation of a good God, but, thanks to a literal understanding of Genesis, were hostile to its most dynamic manifestation, sexuality, as well as to woman, who made it possible and tempting. Gnostics, on the other hand, considered the phenomenal world to be the creation of the inferior, foolish demiurge, whom they identified with the god of the Old Testament. Nevertheless, matter contained spiritual seeds or sparks which needed to be discovered and liberated before the mystery of conjunction between Christos and Ecclesia could be consummated. One view characteristic of many Gnostics, was that sex was permissible and even beneficial to those who understood its symbolic significance i.e. the restoration of the essential androgynous unity of being that existed before the Fall. For Catholics, on the other hand, who, as seen by Gnostics, literalized everything, and were still intent on fruitfully multiplying, the use of sex merely compounded the original demiurgic error. To Gnostics, seeking freedom from error, ignorance and unconsciousness, but little concerned with moralizing notions of sin, it was procreation which was the mistake, not copulation, which some sects practised freely as part of their public religious observance.

The word 'whore' has come down in the world, like many another pertaining to female sexuality, and at first meant probably no more or less than 'lover'. This prejudice against female sexual expression stems from Judaism, always on guard in case the temples of Astarte and her hierodules should lure the faithful into apostasy, and from its successor, mainstream Christianity. Christ himself seems to have been well-disposed towards women. He pardoned the woman taken in adultery and cast seven devils out of Mary Magdalene. Jesus himself comes from a long line of wise whores, according to the Gospel which St Matthew called 'the book of the genealogy of Jesus Christ'. One, Tamar, dresses as a harlot and sits in the gateway to seduce her father-in-law, Judah. A later Tamar, the daughter of David, was raped by her brother. The second ancestress, Rahab, mother of Boaz, bears the same name as the harlot of Jericho, through whose wisdom the Israelites were able to enter and take possession of the Holy Land. She is also the fabulous sea-monster from whose body the world was fashioned and, in Psalm 87, a synonym for Egypt. Ruth, a Moabite, at her mother-in-law's instigation, seduced Boaz, who was an elderly relative of her late husband's as well as Rahab's son. The elders bless his marriage with the words 'may your house be like the house of Perez, whom Tamar bore to Judah.' Bathsheba, wife of a goddess-worshipping Hittite, is mentioned only obliquely: 'And David was the father of Solomon by the wife of Uriah.' Finally there is Mary herself, who was the object of scandalous gossip among the opponents of Christianity. She was accused of being a hairdresser who turned away from her husband and bore Jesus to her paramour, Pandira. In Alexandria the story went that she conceived Jesus by her brother. To the Gnostics, however, the archon Christ was the offspring of Sophia (Wisdom) and Bythos (Depth).

MARY MAGDALENE

The Gnostics, we have already seen, venerated the Magdalen as the favourite disciple, who experienced the highest Gnosis of the redeemer. It is related in the 'Panarion' of Epiphanius that Jesus took Mary with him to a mountain, where he produced a woman from his side and had intercourse with her 'until the semen flowed freely' to show what should be done 'that we might have life'. This demonstration, reminiscent of tantric yoga, no doubt symbolized the engendering of wholeness through union with one's contrasexual 'other half'. In the 'Gospel of Mary' she expounds to the apostles at Peter's request what is hidden from them in the words of the Saviour. Her speech, much of which is missing, shows that she is still in touch with Christ through visions, and discloses that it is in the mind, an intermediate area between soul and spirit, that visions are received. Peter angrily rejects her teaching and is rebuked by Levi: 'Peter, you have always been hot-tempered. Now I see you contending against the woman like the adversaries. But if the Saviour made her worthy, who are you to reject her? Surely the Saviour knows her very well. That is why he loved her more than us.'

Few biographical details can be deduced about Mary from the Bible or the Gnostic writings, but this has not prevented a wealth of material from coming down to us. The main source is the Blessed James of Voragine (c.1230–c.1298), Dominican Archbishop of Genoa and author of The Golden Legend, for centuries a best-selling 'lives of the saints'. His feast-day falls fortuitously on 13 July, the day on which black Sara the Egyptian, who accompanied Mary to France, is also celebrated.

According to Voragine, Mary was of royal blood, the daughter of Syrus (Syrian) and Eucharia (from eucharis, 'gracious' — a term applied to Aphrodite). She, her brother, Lazarus, and her sister, Martha, owned seven castles, in addition to the village of Bethany and much of Jerusalem. Her own dwelling of choice was Magdala (tower), a mile from Gennesaret on the Sea of

Galilee. The only place of this name mentioned in the Bible is Migdol in Exodus 14.2. Here, near the sea — Reed or Red — the Israelites camped for the last time on Egyptian soil before God destroyed Pharaoh's army and Mary the prophetess led a dance of triumph.

It was near Magdala that Jesus questioned Peter about the quality of his love and said to him concerning John, the beloved disciple, 'If I will that he tarry till I come, what is that to thee?' Mary and John, the two beloved of the Lord, had been engaged to be married and the celebrations were actually in progress in Cana when John broke it off to follow Jesus instead. Mary was so chagrined that she threw herself into a life of promiscuity. She was freed from this at a dinner party given by Simon the leper, when Jesus cast seven devils out of her. She and Jesus then became close friends and he defended her against charges of impurity (the Pharisees), laziness (Martha) and extravagance (Judas and the Jews). He stayed with her at Bethany, where her tears over the apparent death of Lazarus, another beloved disciple, moved him to weep.

The leading role played by Mary at the Crucifixion and Resurrection needs no re-telling. Fourteen years after the Ascension, most of which time she spent with the mother of Jesus and, presumably, St John, she was put to sea by the Jews in a leaky boat without oars or rudder, accompanied by her servant, Martilla, who had once called to Jesus, 'blessed is the womb that bore you and the breasts that gave you suck' (Luke 11.27). Other passengers included Cedonius, a blind man healed by Jesus; Maximinus, one of the 72 whose feast-day, 8 June, coincides with that of St Melania (black) and precedes that of St Pelagia (a penitent whore); Lazarus, Martha, Mary Salome, Mary the mother of James, and Sara the black Egyptian servant.

They landed at Ratis, later Les Saintes-Maries-de-la-Mer, and Mary preached against idolatry in the neighbourhood of Marseilles. The ruler of the country came to pray to the idols for a child. Mary dissuaded him and appeared to his wife in a dream on three successive nights threatening the wrath of God unless the saints were looked after. The wife then became pregnant and the ruler set off with her and the new-born baby to discover whether Peter preached the same truth as Mary Magdalene, on whom he bestowed all his worldly goods. During the voyage his wife died, and, after praying to the Magdalen, the ruler left her on a hill with the baby, covering them with his cloak. He then journeyed on to Jerusalem where St Peter took him on a tour of the city. Two years later he returned to the hillside where he found the baby alive, still sucking its dead mother's milk. He prayed once more to the Magdalen and his wife was restored to life. They returned to Marseilles and were baptised by Maximinus who became the first bishop of Aix. Lazarus was created the first bishop of Marseilles and Martha settled in Tarascon (qv) where she quelled the Tarasque, the dragon of the Rhône.

Mary, after her life of activity, decided to choose that better part that was her due and retired to Ste Baume, a name that recalls the holy balm with which long ago she had anointed the body of the Lord. There in a grotto she spent the last thirty years of her earthly existence in prayer and solitude, where the rising sun looks west over Aix and Marseilles. She was buried at St Maximin, where, from the early fifth century, Cassianite monks from St Victor of Marseilles were the guardians of her tomb. Thus the cult is ancient, although many of the relics confirming the legend were not discovered until the thirteenth and fifteenth centuries. Those that were at St Maximin were transferred during the Saracen invasions to Vézelay, which then became one of the sacred high places of the west. Thence her cult spread to ever more Madeleines, whose number increased from 33 to 125 between the eighth and twelfth centuries. Some fifty centres of the cult of the Magdalen also contain shrines to the Black Virgin.

How are we to interpret this story? It hardly requires the eye of faith to see, in the seven demons and the seven castles, the planetary stages on the journey of the soul into and out of incarnation, according to the religion of Ishtar/Astarte/Ashtoreth, a teaching which was assimilated by some Gnostic groups. Astarte, among her many roles, is the goddess of love, in whose temples sexual rites were performed. One clue to the possible identity of the Magdalen in Gnostic eyes is to be found in her parentage. If we put together Syrus and Eucharia (Aphrodite) what we get is Dea Syria, Atargatis, a form of Ishtar, who was worshipped with doves and fishes. If Mary Magdalene was not herself a priestess or initiate of Astarte, then the tradition she represents, closer to John than Peter, may be seen as a syncretistic and esoteric one, thoroughly congenial to the Gnostic outlook.

To Gnostics there was one all-embracing feminine wisdom, including both the virgin and the whore, which they called Sophia or the Holy Spirit. They identified her with the vision granted to John on Patmos of 'a woman clothed with the sun, and the moon under her feet, and upon her head a crown of twelve stars' (Revelation 12.1) and they invoked her as 'Lady'. Later the Cathars, who used the name of John to signify the neophyte undergoing initiation in their rituals, were accused by the Inquisition of using the term 'Our Lady' to refer to their own church of love and to the Holy Spirit. The only parts of the Bible which they accepted were some of the prophetic books and the writings of John, especially Revelation.

Catharism, whose symbols included doves, fishes and a star, was brutally repressed, but ideas cannot be killed. Even when apparently dead and abandoned, like the Princess of Marseilles, the eternal religion of the great feminine spirit continues to nourish its children. An illustration from the Sforza Book of Hours (1490) speaks mutely of such a faith. It shows, in the sky, the huge figure of the Magdalen, as penitent, with hair completely covering her down to her bare feet. Apart from four angels attending her at each corner, like the 'World' in the Tarot, the picture contains a boat whose occupants gaze up in wonder at the heavenly portent, as does a bearded man in prayer on the land. Finally there is a rocky, brown mountain with a cave, outside which are a woman and child.

According to Runciman, the only Occultist child of what he calls 'Christian Dualism', i.e. Catharism, is probably to be found in the symbolism of the Tarot, which appeared in northern Italy, Marseilles and Lyons in the fourteenth century, after the repression of the Cathars and the Templars. There is, however, one other arcane tradition that has recently come to light, which is relevant to our story, that of the Holy Blood and the Holy Grail. Not all Cathars perished after the fall, in 1244, of Montségur, under what they called Mount Tabor, after the Gnostic mountain of the Holy Spirit. Le Roy Ladurie has shown that, up to eighty years later, they were still living their religion in an extensive area of the eastern Pyrenees. Apart from

Montaillou, the greatest concentration of Cathar families was to be found between Arques, source of one of the two major Parisian Black Virgins, Notre-Dame de Paix, and Limoux, home of the black Notre-Dame de Marceille. A mile or so from Arques stands the village 'of Rennes-le-Château, former Visigothic capital of the region, where the most curious cult of Mary Magdalene has its centre. The church there, not, presumably, the first, was dedicated to her in 1059 shortly after the Razès had been acquired by the Counts of Toulouse, at a time when Catharism was beginning to sweep through Europe like wildfire. It was to Rennes, as we have noted, that Sigebert IV came with Merovée Lévi on 17 January 681 to seek refuge at the court of his Visigothic relations. He thus perpetuated the Merovingian blood-line, which, according to Baigent *et al.* stemmed from the union of Jesus Christ and Mary Magdalene.

The church was lavishly rebuilt at the expense of the Abbé Saunière, who was priest of Rennes-le-Château from 1885 to his death in 1917. Such was his veneration for the Magdelen that he also built for himself a large villa which he called Bethania, and a neo-Gothic fort, the Tour Magdala, which he intended using as a library. Some time in the nineteenth century the name of a spring at Rennes-les-Bains, below his tower, was changed from La Gode (the Gothic woman, a title of Freyja — cf. Daroca, Spain) to La Madeleine. Perhaps this alteration was the inspiration of the Abbé Boudet (1831–1915), Saunière's mentor and the author of *La vraie langue celtique*. Deloux and Brétigny mention another spring called La Madeleine in the churchyard of Rennes-le-Château which weeps drop by drop like the fountain of St Germaine, which heals afflictions of the eyes, outside Notre-Dame de Marceille.

The interior of the church offers many surprises. At the entrance, a winged, horned demon, Asmodeus, with a red body and a green dress, holds the water-stoup on his shoulders. (It was Asmodeus, son of Lilith, who tricked Solomon out of his ring of wisdom, through which he knew the language of birds, but it was fortunately returned, like that of Orval, by a fish.) He specialized, like the North African Lilith, Karina, in preventing intercourse between newly-weds, and, in the Book of Tobit, after killing seven of Sara's husbands on their wedding-nights, was finally banished to Egypt by Tobias, by means of a fish's liver. The other church in France where I have seen a modern coloured image of a single devil is that of Stenay (Satanacum), Merovingian stronghold and shrine near Orval, whence Sigebert, escaping his father's assassins, set out on his long journey. Curiously, in one of the statues of Jesus in the church, his posture, kneeling on one knee, eyes and face cast down sideways, is a mirror image of Asmodeus. In place of the holy water stoup, a baptismal vessel is held above his head by John.

The other contents of the church at Rennes merit no less attention. To begin with, many of the saints we shall shortly be discussing as companions of the Black Virgin and favourites of the Prieuré are represented. St Roch, like Amfortas the Fisher King, points to the unstanchable wound in his thigh. St Germaine Cousin de Pibrac releases a shower of roses from her apron, symbolizing, perhaps, the descendants of the Magdalen's womb who continue to flourish, against all odds, through the generations. There is a second statue of Jesus preaching from a mountain-top, which, like St Germaine's apron, is cascading with roses. St Anthony the Hermit from the sacred masonic city of Memphis, who overcame hallucinatory temptations in the desert, no doubt owes his place at Rennes to the coincidence of his feast-day, 17 January, with the arrival of Sigebert at Rennes. He is holding a closed book, signifying a mystery, possibly a stage in the alchemical process. His namesake, St Anthony of Padua (qv), invoked for finding that which is lost, and usually depicted holding a child, carries in his hand a fleur-de-lys, symbol since Merovingian times of the French royal family, and the flower which grows outside the Grail Castle. There are two images of the Magdalen, one holding a vase, perhaps containing balm or ashes, and one, under the altar, which shows her praying outside a cave. In a unique arrangement the Virgin Mary, here called 'the Virgin Mother', is carrying a child on one side of the choir, while St Joseph carries a second one on the other side. Against the exterior wall of the church a stucco statue of Our Lady of Lourdes is placed on top of a magnificent Visigothic pillar. The decoration of the lintel, which consists of crosses and roses, may point to a Rosicrucian influence.

ST BERNARD OF CLAIRVAUX

If Rennes-le-Château provides striking testimony to the persistence of the tradition still linking the Merovingian blood-line to Mary Magdalene, what of Vézelay (qv), the great centre of her cult in the Middle Ages? It was there, on Easter Sunday 1146, in front of King Louis VII, his troubadour queen, Eleanor, and some 100,000 nobles, knights and commoners, that St Bernard preached the Second Crusade. The great basilica of St Mary Magdalene was begun in 1096, the year of the First Crusade, when Godefroy de Bouillon set forth to claim the Kingdom of Jerusalem that was his by divine right. In 1217, Francis of Assisi, the troubadour saint of love and peace who, according to Runciman, caught something of the Cathar spirit and doctrine in his teachings, founded at Vézelay the first house of his Order in France. His Cordeliers and Capuchins are sometimes guardians of the Black Virgin.

Much has already been written about St Bernard in the Introduction. There can be little doubt that he plays a vital part in our story, as he did in almost all that happened in the twelfth century. He was deeply involved in the politics of his time, which was largely concerned with the relations of Church and State and the possibilities of uniting Christendom. Descendant of knights who had fought the infidel in Spain, Bernard, as a romantic boy, would have responded strongly to stories of the First Crusade and the vision of great armies setting forth from Clermont and Le Puy with the 'Salve Regina' on their lips. His uncle was one of the original nine Templars who spent nine years in Jerusalem on their enigmatic mission. On their return Bernard wrote the rule of their order and commended to them the 'obedience of Bethany, the Castle of Mary and Martha'. Meantime he had taken over the ailing young Cistercian Order and turned it into a power-house of civilization. Whatever his vision for Christendom, it seems to have included a unity in which Pope and Emperor each had his part to play, with the Kingdom of Jerusalem providing a symbolic rallying-point. Vast multi-national corporations like the Benedictines, Cistercians and Templars provided the infrastructure vital to the unity, efficiency and progress of Europe.

It is, however, as a great saint and mystic rather than as a statesman or polemist that Bernard is chiefly remembered today. He attached much importance to safeguarding Jerusalem, capital of Godefroy de Bouillon, but his real goal was the spiritual Sion, the bride of God, where lasting treasure can alone be found. In one of the many letters he wrote to Queen Mélisande, daughter, wife and mother of Kings of Jerusalem, Bernard advised: 'The Queen of the South came to hear the wisdom of Solomon to learn to be ruled and to rule in the same fashion. Now there is one greater than Solomon. Abandon yourself then to the Lord of Sion.' The heart of Bernard's spirituality is his devotion to Jesus as lover of the soul, a devotion that even today has a steamy, erotic quality that is somewhat shocking. 'I do not want your blessing, it is you I want,' he cries to the one he referred to as 'the husband' or 'the Word'. It is for this reason that the passionate, poetic imagery of the Song of Solomon is so much to his taste, as, identifying himself in soul with the black Shulamite, he abandons himself to the spiritual caresses of the divine lover.

The joys of spiritual love are androgynous, and it was no contradiction for Bernard to be also the greatest cavalier, servant and votary of Our Lady. In a prayer for the Nativity of the Virgin, 8 September 1308, addressed to 'Saint Mary, Holy Mother of God', the Templars awaiting death at Chinon besought her: 'Defend your religion which was founded by your holy and dear confessor, the Blessed Bernard' (Roy, p.235). Bernard's love of Notre Dame goes hand in hand with his dislike of the modernist, rationalizing tendencies which he attacked in the theology of his day, especially in Abelard. It also accords with a tendency towards nature mysticism: 'You will find more things in forests than in books; the trees, the stones will teach you what the masters cannot. Do you think that you cannot suck honey from the stone, oil from the hardest rock? Do the mountains not distil sweetness? Are the hills not flowing with milk and honey? There is so much I could tell you. I can hardly stop myself' (Letter 106). Is this a memory of his boyhood at Châtillon, with its woods, hills and springs, where he tasted the sweetness that distilled from the breast of the Black Virgin?

Of his other encounters with Black Virgins little is known for sure. He visited Aachen, Clermont-Ferrand, Dijon, Hasselt, Longpont, Paris, Rocadamour, Rome, Toulouse, Tournai and

Valenciennes, in all of which he would certainly have revered Our Lady. The Black Virgin of Affligem returned his 'Ave Maria' with a 'Salve Bernarde' and advised him to get on with his writing. He founded the Abbey of Orval, where the modern Black Virgin may well be continuing an older tradition. His links with Rocadamour are curious. In 1170, seventeen years after Bernard's death, the first document relating to the events there was produced by Robert de Thorigny, Abbot of Mont-Saint-Michel, who also first mentioned the Plantard motto 'Et in Arcadia ego'. In 1166 the Benedictines had found a well-preserved body in a tomb next to the chapel of the Black Virgin, which was claimed to be that of Amador/Zacchaeus/Sylvanus, of Jericho, Sinai and Lucca. He is not mentioned in Butler's five-volume *Lives of the Saints,* but the *Penguin Dictionary of Saints* assigns him as a feast-day 20 August. When Bernard was canonized on 18 January 1175 this also was the day that he was given. Thus, whether consciously or not, the Church emphasized a link between these two lovers of the Black Virgin. The remains of Clairvaux-on-the-Absinthe are now a prison, but in the small village church a painting of the Black Virgin was in a place of veneration when I visited it in 1981.

Bernard no doubt visited Rocamadour on his return from an exhausting and unsuccessful preaching mission against the Cathars of the Toulousain in 1145. He had already advised the use of troops against their co-religionaries in Germany, and would doubtless have pursued a similar course in the Languedoc if the Count of Toulouse had been amenable. But Bernard, too, was a child of his age, and not wholly immune to the spirit which favoured the Cathar phenomenon. Like the Gnostics, he based his spirituality on direct experience rather than on syllogisms. In the chastity which is the sign of absolute fidelity to God and Notre Dame, he is indistinguishable from a Cathar parfait. He wrote: 'God lives where continence endures. Chastity unites man to God. Continence makes man very close to God.' René Nelli has pointed out that this last proposition figures almost word for word in the Cathar ritual.

Apart from his orthodox detestation of Catharism, as a doctrine, though he admired the parfaits, Bernard must have found it a thorn in the flesh, hindering the great plan, spreading disunity among nations, attacking the Church in the rear, weakening it and bringing it into disrepute. It is not impossible that, faced with such an obstacle, irremovable by either political or religious means, Bernard should try to beat the Cathars at their own game. Dominic and Francis were to try much the same tactic — being just as holy, chaste, self-denying and poor as the parfaits. To reforge Christian Europe in the twelfth century, however, the piety of Bernard's Cistercians was not enough. The whole people of God needed to be inspired to lead the symbolic life. Such an inspiration was found from two sources — the building of the great Gothic cathedrals under the impetus of the new Templar/Cistercian architectural principles, and the making of pilgrimages. On the long route to Compostela, festooned with Black Virgin churches, between 500,000 and 2 million pilgrims journeyed every year. A Poitevin monk, Aimeri Picard, published a tourist guide of the various itineraries to Compostela in 1130, with the sights to see on the way. Benedictine and Cistercian guest-houses were placed at easy stages along the various roads, which were guarded by Templars and the other military orders. If the Cathars, beset by foes all round, made their religion even more mysterious than Gnosticism always is to the rational and orthodox, why not take the wind out of their sails? One means might be gently to promote the mystery of the Black Virgin, throned in the crypts and chancels of new churches rich in enigmatic carvings that expressed the inner pilgrimage. If such was the idea, it was only partly successful. Some of the guardians of the faith themselves, Templars, Franciscans and Dominicans, perhaps influenced by the power of the symbols they contemplated in their chapels, were visited by strange ideas and individual revelations. For the simple people, on the other hand, the Black Virgin no doubt continued to be what she had been for some thirty millennia, the manifestation of the Great Goddess.

CATHARS, TEMPLARS AND THE GRAIL

The following is a summary of the important connections, some of which have already been referred to, that can be made between Cathars, Templars, the Holy Grail and the cult of the Black Virgin.

1 Both Cathars and Templars were reputed to be the guardians or possessors of the Grail.

2 The last guardian of the Grail, Prester John, the nephew of Parzival, called himself the Priest-King of India and Ethiopia and probably represents an eastern Manichaean or Nestorian tradition. Through Ethiopia there is a connection with Solomon, the Queen of Sheba and the Ark of the Covenant.

3 Both Cathars and Templars were accused by the Inquisition of denying the validity of the sacraments, of renouncing the Cross, and of sodomy. The same Dominican inquisitor, Bernard Gui, went straight from oppressing Cathars in Toulouse to torturing Templars in Chinon and Paris.

4 Both had special extra-ecclesial rites which they kept secret, and avoided the priests and practices of conventional Christianity.

5 The Templars refused to take part in the Albigensian Crusade and, on occasion, offered Cathars refuge. They may even locally have taken up arms for the Cathar cause. Many Cathars became Templars at that time.

6 The Templars were particularly strong in the Cathar regions (e.g. two important Templar houses within three miles of Rennes-le-Château) and hoped to create a Templar state consisting of Provence, Languedoc, Aquitaine, Roussillon, Catalonia, Navarre, Majorca and Aragon, whose rulers were generally sympathetic to both Templars and Cathars. Black Virgins are numerous in these regions.

7 According-to Charpentier, the Templars' spirituality was inspired by the mysteries of Egypt and they themselves were distant descendants of the Valentinian Gnostics of Alexandria.

8 The two centuries during which Cathars and Templars flourished and declined almost exactly coincide. Most Black Virgins date from this period (1100-1300), as does the cult of the Holy Grail.

9 A considerable proportion of Black Virgins are reputed to have been brought back from the Crusades, many by Templars.

10 Cathars and Templars both maintained secret contacts with

eastern heterodox religious groups, as well as with Jews and Arabs.

11 The troubadour movement, also repressed by the Church, forms a link between Cathars, Templars and the Grail.

12 The Cathar symbolism of figures with disproportionately large hands is a common feature of Black Virgins.

13 The great festival of the Templars was Pentecost, day of the Holy Spirit, as opposed to Easter or Christmas. Pentecost is also the high feast of the Arthurian Grail legends. The Cathars saw the coming of Jesus as just a stage, prefiguring the coming of the Holy Spirit.

14 Four hermaphrodite Gnostic statues, which had been discovered in Templar houses in or near Vienna, came to light there during the second decade of the nineteenth century, and were for a time in the Imperial Museum.

15 Both the Holy Grail and the Templar Baphomets (heads with one, two or three faces) protected, nourished and brought fertility to the land. The Black Virgin has similar powers. The Baphomet was said by the Templars to be 'the principle of beings created by God Trinity'. It has also been seen as the symbol of divine wisdom and Hugh J. Schonfield has demonstrated that, in the Hebrew Atbash cipher, Baphomet converts to Sophia. One of the few Baphomets ever discovered was the head of a woman. Girart de Marsac, on becoming a Templar, was shown a small image of a woman and was told that all would go well for him if he put his trust in her.

16 According to one legend, the lead Grail vessel containing the holy blood of Christ was washed up on the shore at Fécamp, where it hung from a fig-tree and worked miracles. Perhaps, like the lead coffin of Osiris, which suffered a similar fate, it is the real secret of alchemy. Mary Magdalene's arrival in France might be seen in a similar light.

17 The Order of the Temple was reputedly the creation of the Prieuré Notre-Dame de Sion, the guardian of the Merovingian blood-line and deeply involved in the cult of the Black Virgin.

SOME SAINTS OF THE HIDDEN ORDER

St Dagobert (651-79)
Dagobert II, son of Sigebert III of Austrasia and grand-son of 'le bon roi Dagobert I', last Merovingian king of all the Franks, was born in 651, heir to his father's throne. On the latter's death in 656, Dagobert was abducted by the usurping Mayor of the Palace, Grimoald, and entrusted to the Bishop of Poitiers, who took him to Ireland and left him at the monastery of Slane. He married a Celtic princess and was able to convince St Wilfrid of York by 'certain signs' that he was indeed the rightful king. His first wife died in 670, giving birth to their third daughter and he remarried Giselle de Razès, niece of the King of the Visigoths, at her home, Rennes-le-Château. In 676, their son Sigebert was born, and, soon after, he established himself on the throne, in his capital, Stenay. On 23 December 679 at midday, while resting at the foot of a tree during a hunt in the nearby Forest of Woevre, he was lanced through the eye by his godson, under the orders of Pepin of Heristal, and killed. Sigebert IV, it was alleged, was rescued and taken to Rennes-le-Château.

Dagobert was the first king of France to be canonized, two centuries after his death, in the reign of Charles the Bald, and a church was dedicated to him at Stenay. A verse account of his martyrdom in Latin was discovered at the Abbey of Orval (qv) in the mid-nineteenth century. His feast-day 23 December, also belongs, according to Robert Graves, to Benjamin, 'The Ruler of the South', whose totem animal is the wolf. It is also the beginning of the Saturnalia. Dagobert receives no entry in the dictionaries of saints and no trace of him is on public view at Stenay.

Ste Roseline de Villeneuve (1263-1329)
Ste Roseline's feast-day, 17 January, is also the great date in the calendar of the Merovingian blood-line. Indeed, her very name may symbolize that line. She was the daughter of Arnold of Villeneuve and Sibylle de Sabran. The Arnold of Villanova or Villeneuve known to history was a Catalan alchemist, mystic and physician (1240-1311), who knew the secret of sweetening the soluble salt of the sea, which was known in the art as the Virgin Mary or Stella Maris. Saint-Sabran was the quarter of

Toulouse associated with La Reine Pédauque, whose mother was called Rosala. Roseline had a brother, Helios, an unusual name evocative of the sun-god, Elijah and Lohengrin, who is sometimes called Helias. He was a crusader whom Roseline miraculously freed from his prison on the island of Rhodes (see Pézenas). As with Ste Germaine at Rennes, and other saints, a miracle of roses is attributed to her. Her body lies in the chapel near her family castle of Les Arcs (!) in Provence. It was so incorrupt, even to the brightness of the eyes, that Louis XIV, during a visit, ordered his physician to stick a needle into the left pupil, which still bears the marks. Perhaps in thus re-enacting the martyrdom of Dagobert, the Sun-King was taking the unconscious vengeance of a monarch of dubious rights on a symbol of the true blood-line. Deloux and Brétigny consider that Ste Roseline is Gerard de Nerval's 'Queen of the South'.

St Sulpice (d. c.647)

This contemporary of St Dagobert also has his feast day on 17 January. He was the second Bishop of Bourges, which is on the zero meridian of Paris, like Rennes-les-Bains, and was successful in converting all the Jews of his diocese. He was the protégé of the goldsmith St Eloi, Grand Vizier of Dagobert I. The famous seminary and church dedicated to him in Paris contains the obelisk with the copper line down the centre marking the exact point of the meridian. St Sulpice, in the grounds of St Germain-des-Prés (qv), had connections with the Prieuré from its foundation in 1642. (See also Villefranche-de-Conflent *et passim*.)

St Vincent de Paul (c.1580-1660)

Monsieur Vincent is a famous historical figure whose life abounds in enigmas. He left his flocks in the Landes and studied for the priesthood in Toulouse. In 1605, five years after ordination, he borrowed a horse, sold it and disappeared for two years. During that period he claimed to have been captured by Barbary pirates near Marseilles and sold into slavery in Tunis. One of his owners was an alchemist, whose secrets he seems to have learnt. He awakened to religion a woman, whom he described as a 'natural Turk', who helped him to escape. He set out with a Moslem convert from Nice in a small skiff, and they landed safely at Aigues-Mortes after a voyage of more than 1,000 kilometres. It was not only Molière with his 'que diable allait-il faire dans cette galère?' who found this tale hard to swallow. Deloux and Brétigny have suggested that for Marseilles we should read Marceille, home of the Black Virgin of Limoux, where Vincent met Jean Plantard the Alchemist, Count of Saint-Clair. According to this theory he was taken not to the Barbary coast but to the Chateau de Barberie, near Décize (qv), the 'occult bastion of France' and seat of the Merovingian descendants since the tenth century. It was utterly destroyed on the orders of Cardinal Mazarin in 1659. To complete this tale told in the *langue des oiseaux,* for 'les Maures' (Moors), who captured Vincent as alleged in his letter to M. de Comet, we could understand 'les morts' (the dead), indicating the death and rebirth initiation he must have undergone.

Those two years had an electrifying effect on the career of this poor priest with no connections and a dubious reputation for horse-trading and extravagant traveller's tales. In 1608 he journeyed to Rome where he reputedly demonstrated alchemical processes to the Pope, before returning to France on a secret mission to King Henry IV. He was taken up by Cardinal Bérulle, who arranged a good post for him with the family of Emmanuel de Gondi, Director-General of the Galleys. In 1617 he went to Bourg-en-Bresse (qv), where he has a chapel in the Church of the Black Virgin, and evangelized the countryside. On his return he became confessor to the Queen, Anne of Austria, and attended her husband Louis XIII on his death-bed. A fresco in his chapel in St Sulpice shows the Queen at the foot of the bed comforting two children, while Vincent, at the head, points the dying king to heaven. The problem is that Queen Anne had only one child, the future Louis XIV, whose 'miraculous' birth after twenty-three years of fruitless marriage gave rise to much ribald speculation concerning his legitimacy ('was Richelieu or Mazarin the father?'). It also gravely disappointed the hopes of the House of Lorraine, the claimants to the throne who represented the Merovingian blood-line.

If the mysterious second child stands for the 'lost king', ever ready and waiting to assume the throne, perhaps this is also how we may interpret the lost child with whom St Vincent is sometimes shown in iconography. He certainly seems to have had the interests of the blood-line at heart. A disciple of his was J.-J. Olier, the founder of the Society of St Sulpice, who had been healed of blindness and loss of faith by the Black Virgin of Loreto. He and Olier were the two clerical heads of the Compagnie du Saint-Sacrement along with Nicholas Pavillon, Jansenist Bishop of Alet, a town half-way between Rennes-le-Château and Limoux. This secret society, or 'cabale des dévots', satirized by Molière in *Tartuffe* was, it has been suggested, the form taken by the Prieuré to further the interests of the blood-line between 1627 and 1667, in opposition to the policies of Mazarin.

In 1633 St Vincent received from the Canons of St Victor the Priory of St Lazarus, which became his home and the mother house of the new congregation he founded to care for the needy, especially orphans and galley-slaves. He called it his Noah's Ark. The Missionaries of St Vincent de Paul were placed in charge of the pilgrimage to the Black Virgin of Marceille in 1873, and a large stone statue of their founder still bears mute testimony to his extraordinary career. St Vincent is known to have had a fervent devotion to both extant major Black Virgins in Paris. Notre-Dame de Paix, which was once the possession of the Joyeuse family at Arques, was made the object of a forty-days' indulgence in 1642 by Jean-François de Gondi, the first Archbishop of Paris and the brother of Vincent's patron. An illustration of the scene shows St Vincent praying in paradise on the same level as Our Lady, half-way between God and the people of France. He entrusted all his multifarious projects to Notre-Dame de Bonne Délivrance and it was planned that his body should make a station in the Chapel of the Black Virgin in 1806. A medal was struck to commemorate this event which never took place, with the Virgin on one side and a bust of St Vincent on the other. The Virgin made her final home in the Boulevard d'Argenson, family name of a well-known member of the Compagnie du Saint-Sacrement and author of its annals.

There are some sequences of saints' days that seem to have a special significance within the context of the hidden order. For instance, the feast day of St Vincent de Paul, 19 July, inaugurates an interesting octave: 20 July, St Margaret or Marina, 21 July, St Victor of Marseilles; 22 July, St Mary Magdalene, 23 July, St John Cassian, founder of St Victor de Marseilles (also the

Roman Neptūnalia); 24 July, St Loup of Troyes; 25 July, St Christopher, a Canaanite giant and devil-worshipper, and St James the Greater (Santiago); 26 July, St Anne.

Gerbert of Aurillac, Pope Sylvester II (c.940-1003)

Although this unorthodox and Gnosticizing Pope exuded the odour of sanctity from his incorrupt body, he was never raised to the altars of the Church. The first Frenchman to be Pope, he acceded to the throne of Peter in 999, fortunate inversion of 666, the number of the Great Beast, at a time when the world was awaiting the dreaded millennium. He had much in common with St Vincent de Paul. Both were poor shepherds of Aquitaine, though from opposite corners of the province. Each had a liberating experience with a pagan woman and was apprenticed to an alchemist during an alleged journey to the world of Islam. On their return, both rapidly rose to positions of decisive importance in Church and State.

Gerbert was born in Aurillac, home of a Black Virgin and of a golden statue of St Géraud whose idolatrous splendour rivalled that of St. Foy de Conques (qv). Aurillac was noted for its golden fleeces, sheepskins left in the River Jordanne to attract particles of gold, and for its strong, ancient links with Compostela. The Benedictines of St Géraud, recognizing Gerbert's genius, sent him to study mathematics at Vich in Catalonia, on the road to Compostela, and other subjects at the great Arab universities of Toledo and Cordoba. According to one legend, he seduced the daughter of his alchemist master in order to learn the secret of secrets and was expelled from Spain. In another version he met a maiden of marvellous beauty, brilliant in gold and tissues of silk, who told him her name was Meridiana ('lady of the south'), and offered him her body, her riches and her magical wisdom if he would trust her. Gerbert agreed to the bargain and in a short time became successively Archbishop of Rheims, where Clovis was anointed, Archbishop of Ravenna, where Mérovée spent his youth, and Pope. As well as being the first Christian alchemist, credited with achieving the great work, he also had a talking head, which seems to have operated like a primitive computer. He introduced Arabic numbers to the west and invented the clock, the astrolabe and the hydraulic organ. In the realm of politics, he attempted to raise a crusade for the liberation of the Holy Land and established the Church in Hungary, ancient

6. Aurillac

Sicambria, making Stephen its first king. Perhaps the remarkable career of Gerbert is a demonstration that trust is the price demanded by the whore wisdom for her favours.

Ste Colombe and companions

According to Butler's *Lives of the Saints* there are, in addition to the first Abbot of Iona, two female saints called Columba. One, St Columba of Cordoba, the great centre of eastern Jewry in Arabic Spain, was a nun beheaded by the Moors in 853. Her feast-day, 17 September, coincides with that of St Hildegard of Bingen, 'the Sibyl of the Rhine', who corresponded at length with St Bernard. The following day belongs to St Thomas of

Villeneuve or Villanova, who curiously has a second feast on 22 September. That is also the feast of St Maurice (who has his individual feast on 21 July, the day before the Magdalen) and his companions, including Ursus ('bear') and Victor. Maurice, a Manichaean from Egypt, held the spear of Longinus until his dying breath to keep it from the Emperor Maximian. The spear of destiny is the masculine complement to the Holy Grail. Following Maurice's example 6,666 legionaries died with him, without offering resistance. Thomas of Villeneuve, with whose Sisters the Black Virgin of Paris resides, cares especially for lost children and was Bishop of the Grail city of Valencia. His views on the encounter of the Magdalen with the risen Christ are identical to those of St Bernard. He shares his first feast with St Methodius of Tyre (city of King Hiram, master mason of the Temple) or of Olympus (abode of the gods), who wrote a hymn to Christ as bridegroom of the Church. 19 September sees the feast of St Januarius of the famous liquefying holy blood, once preserved at Monte Vergine (qv), which is the pride of Naples (qv), fief of the Anjou dynasty. The two following days belong respectively to the wild huntsman St Eustace, patron of Madrid, whose relics are at St Denis, and St Maura, a dark lady from Troyes. 21 September is, however, better known as the feast of St Matthew, author of Christ's genealogy.

The second Ste Colombe is a virgin martyr from Sens, whose feast-day 31 December, which looks back to the old year and forward to the new, is shared with St Melania (the black) and St Sylvester. Perhaps it is she who gave her name to a village on the Seine, a mile away from St Bernard's Châtillon.

Who then is the Ste Colombe referred to in *Nostra* (March/April 1983)? She apparently crossed the Pyrenees from Spain, accompanied by a bear, and settled first at Colombiès in Aveyron, near Rodez (qv), a village on the zero meridian. She was nourished for twenty-eight days by manna, served on a miraculous shield, before making her home at Finestret, where her church contains a Black Virgin and, above the porch, a statue of the saint and her bear. A second village of Ste Colombe, some twenty miles to the north-east, just the other side of the meridian, attests to her fame in the eastern Pyrenees, where the cult of the Black Virgin is widespread. Her own cult was fostered by St Sulpice of Bourges, whence, according to de Sède, two

Princes, Bellovesus and Segovesus, set out to conquer the world *c*.400 BC. The first founded Milan (Mediolanum) and sacked Rome. The second led to the east an army of Volscian Tectosages from Toulouse. Their descendants sacked Delphi and founded Galatia.

The authors of *The Holy Blood and the Holy Grail* report a recent visit by members of the Prieuré 'to one of Sion's sacred sites, the village of Sainte-Colombe near Nevers, where the Plantard domain of Chateau Barberie was situated'.

The dove (*colombe*), the symbol of both Venus and the Holy Spirit, is the bird which brought La Sainte Ampoulle, the vessel that contained the oil used to anoint the Kings of France. In astronomy the constellation Columba flies just ahead of the ship Argo. Joseph is chosen by Mary among a host of suitors, when a dove flies from his rod and lands on his head.

St Roch and companions

One of the saints whose statue is most frequently found accompanying the Black Virgin is St Roch (Rock). This is surprising, since, at his death in 1327, aged about 32, most of the Romanesque Black Virgins had long been installed in their shrines. He was born in Montpellier in what had been Visigothic Septimania, in the shadow of Notre-Dame des Tables, after his mother, Liberia, prayed to La Nègre. He travelled as a healer in northern Italy, the main centre of Catharism at the time, caught the plague in Piacenza, recovered and was imprisoned as a spy. He also found time to make the pilgrimage to Compostela. According to another account he returned home and was imprisoned there when his relatives failed to recognize him. After his death, a miraculous cross was found imprinted on his body, similar to one of the physical signs by which the Merovingian blood-line can be recognized. In iconography he is almost always accompanied by a dog, the animal of Hecate, Hermes and Tobias. His other symbol is the terrible wound to which he points on the upper thigh, reminiscent of the Fisher-King's. St James is shown with such a wound in a painting at Santiago de Compostela. In 1913 the Church superimposed on his feast, 16 August, the day after Assumption, that of St Joachim, father of the Virgin Mary, who gave his name to the prophet of the coming spiritual church, Joachim of Flora. Saints who are remembered in the week between the Assumption and the Feast of the Immaculate Heart include Sts Bernard, Amadour, Louis d'Anjou, the twin temple-builders, Florus and Laurus, and John Eudes (1601-80). The last was a member of the Oratory, founded by St Vincent de Paul's benefactor, Bérulle, worked with fallen women, and, inspired by the Black Virgin of La Délivrande, founded his own congregation dedicated to the hearts of Jesus and Mary.

If 15 August commemorates the journey to heaven of the great mother of Christ, 18 August celebrates the discoverer of the Cross and the great mother of Christianity, Helen, whose son, Constantine, established it as the religion of the Empire. As the great goddesses of paganism were accompanied by sacrificial son-lovers, so two boy martyrs, Tarsicius and Mamas, whose relics are at Lucca, have their feasts on 15 and 17 August respectively. It is curious that Jacko of Cracow, 17 August, the doughty 'light of Poland', has come down to us as St Hyacinth, name of the beautiful youth slain by Apollo, especially as the Greek *hyakinthos* means 'fleur-de-lys'. (See Arfeuilles, La Chapelle-Geneste, Halle, Mayres, Mende, Meymac, Murat, Ribeauvillé, Saumur, Thuir *et passim*.) At Meymac St Roch's companion is not a dog but a tiny lady in black.

St Blaise

The historical existence of St Blaise is much less likely than that of St Roch. If Roch is the consort of the heavenly Virgin of the Assumption, Blaise accompanies the Lady of the Underworld, whose feast, Candlemas, 2 February, precedes his by one day. His popularity in the west as a saint to be invoked for sick animals and humans is no doubt due in part to the similarity of his name to Blez, a wolf-god identified with Dis, the father of the Gauls. This figure has been called, like Saturn, a sort of earth-mother of the masculine sex. In legend, Blaise forced a wolf to disgorge a poor woman's pig. He also saved the life of a boy by removing a fish-bone from his throat, giving rise to the ritual blessing of the throat still performed today. His symbols are a comb, the instrument of his martyrdom, and two crossed candles similar to St Andrew's saltire and the rune signifying the name of God. After his death, seven women collected his blood. Huynen states that Blaise, Anne, John the Baptist, and Michael are the saints most closely associated with the cult of the Black Virgin (see Blois). Blaise is the name of Merlin's master, who saved him from the Devil, and also his scribe who told the story of the Holy Grail. He was united with the Wardens of the Grail and dwelt thereafter in perpetual joy.

St Brice

St Brice or Britius (d.443) occasionally occurs as a place-name near Black Virgin sites (see Avioth *et passim*). He was a lost child, exposed on the banks of the Loire and rescued by St Martin to whom he was a constant thorn in the flesh. Martin even exclaimed: 'If Christ endured Judas, why not Martin Brice?' He nevertheless succeeded his benefactor as Bishop of Tours, though his pride made him unpopular and he was driven from his see for thirty years on grounds of immorality. Saillens thinks his popularity stems from Briccia, Celtic deity of springs. It is also worth noting that the Bryces of Pannonia, Hungary, who fought Tiberius and defeated Decius, were the ancestors of the Franks. Pyrene, beloved of Hercules, for whom the Pyrenees are named, was the daughter of Bebrycius, aponymous founder of the Bebryces, a powerful tribe in the area. St Brice shares a feast-day, 13 November, with St Bonhomme, the usual designation for a Cathar Parfait. The Cathars fasted from 13 November to Christmas.

Sts Amadour and Veronica

Amadour (lover), eponymous saint of Rocadamour, was born according to legend in Lucca, where his relics are venerated. He was the owner of a field in Sinai where corn miraculously grew to protect the Holy Family from Herod's troops during the flight from Egypt. As Zacchaeus, he was the diminutive publican who climbed a sycamore in Jericho to see Jesus and became his host for dinner and the night. The story of Zacchaeus occurs only in St Luke's Gospel (19.1-10). The old spelling of Lucca is Luca, the Italian for Luke. The passage in which Mary anoints Jesus's feet occurs much earlier in St Luke (7.36) than in the three other gospels. In Luke it comes immediately after the Zacchaeus episode. Matthew and Mark place the dinner-party at the house of Simon the Leper, while to John the setting was Bethany, at the house of Mary and Martha. John specifically mentions that

Lazarus, their brother, whom Jesus had raised from the dead, was at table with them. The next event is the triumphant entry of Jesus into Jerusalem.

We thus see Jesus favouring with his presence an outcast, whether by reason of his leprosy (and Lazarus, too, has come to signify a redeemed leper), or his occupation of tax-collector. This figure is also, by association, a beloved disciple who underwent a death-rebirth initiation and became in legend the first Bishop of Marseilles. The part of this tradition called 'Zacchaeus/Amador' came from the eastern Mediterranean, not to Provence, but to Soulac (qv) near the mouth of the Gironde. Thence he journeyed to Souillac which, like Soulac, means place of wild boars or *solitaires* (one of the physical characteristics peculiar to the Merovingian Kings was a line of bristles, like those of a boar, along the spine). He arrived at length at Rocamadour, whither he was guided by angels to the shrine of Sulevia (Cybele) whom he replaced by a Black Virgin carved by St Luke. His influence extended to the Auvergne (see Billom and St Nectaire). His body, as we have seen, was discovered in 1166 in the cave where he had placed the original Black Virgin. In Berry he was venerated as Silvanus, Latin name for the uncanny god of uncultivated land beyond the village boundaries, a synonym for Faunus/Pan and sometimes for Mars. His first feast-day at Rocamadour was 1 May, the day once sacred to Belen and the May Queen which is now the Feast of St Joseph the Workman. The name Zacchaeus/Zaccai means 'pure', the exact translation of Cathar. In St Luke's version, the man who invited Jesus to dinner on the occasion when a sinful woman of the town anointed the feet of Jesus was Simon the Pharisee. Pharisee also means 'pure'. Amadour has also been associated with the Arabic Amad-Aour, 'the just'.

Zacchaeus travelled to Aquitaine with his wife Veronica. Her name may derive from Verus Iconicus, 'true as of an image'. Lucca was famous for its images of 'the Holy Face of Lucca', Vaudelucques. The Holy Face was that of a black Christ in St Martin's Cathedral, carved by Nicodemus, to whom Jesus revealed the secret of rebirth (John 3.1-21) during a conversation by night. The statue arrived miraculously in Lucca in 782. Veronica is also the name of the saintly maiden who handed her napkin to Jesus on his way to Calvary, and found it imprinted with a true image of the Saviour's face after he had wiped the sweat from his brow. It is now preserved in St Peter's, Rome. Veronica may be the woman with an issue of blood who touched the border of Jesus's garment and was healed at once, although she had been haemorrhaging for twelve years. This story is interpolated in the middle of the miracle of the resuscitation of Jairus's ('God enlightens') daughter (Luke 7.40-56). Only Luke tells us that the girl was twelve years old. Before leaving Veronica of Lucca, let us note that San Frediano or Finnian, from Moville, a sixth-century Irish saint, was Bishop of Lucca in Merovingian times. His feast-day, 10 September, is also that of the Empress Pulcheria, first known possessor of an image of the Virgin, painted by St Luke, the Theotokos Hodegitria, some of whose copies are ranked as Black Virgins. William Rufus, who never broke an oath sworn by the Holy Face of Lucca, was sacrificed, according to Hugh Ross Williamson, in strange circumstances in 1100, at Lammas-tide, 1 August, the feast of Lug/Luc. Ross Williamson considers that the Holy Face of Lucca may be a Cathar devotion (p.33), but also states that Rufus may have been swearing by the Great Bull of paganism. The bull is the animal of St Luke, the reputed painter or sculptor of so many Black Virgins.

Other derivations of Veronica include Berenice, from the Greek 'Pherenike', bringer of victory, one of the attributes of the Virgin herself as Nikopoieon. Berenice was a Jewish princess of the family of Herod, born in AD 28, whom Titus brought to Rome with the intention of marrying, but changed his mind for fear of offending the Romans. Another Berenice was the sister-wife of Ptolemy Euergetes, King of Egypt (247-224 BC). She vowed her hair to the gods to bring her husband victory, but it was stolen from the Temple of Arsinoë at Zephyrium on the first night. Conon of Samos told the king that the winds had blown it to the stars. There it remains as the Coma Berenices, part of the constellation of the Virgin, between the Ox-Driver and the Lion. The corn that hid the Holy Family in Amadour's field during the Flight to Egypt is itself the hair of the Virgin. This scene is depicted at Avioth and in other Black Virgin churches. St Veronica shares a feast, 12 July, with St Nabor, the christianization of Neptune.

Does the story of Amador and Veronica indicate that the pure lover of the Church, not of Roma but Amor, born of the spirit, is wedded to the true image of the good God imprinted within the soul?

SOME HARLOT SAINTS

A number of Egyptian or Levantine harlot saints figure in the Church's calendar alongside Mary Magdalene. Mary the Egyptian is depicted next to her as black in a window of the church of St Merri in Paris and their iconography is sometimes very similar. Mary came to Alexandria in the hope of earning her fare to Jerusalem, where she wished to venerate the true Cross. With this end in view she prostituted herself to sailors for seventeen years before retiring to the desert to live a life of penitence as a hermit, clad in nothing but her hair and progressively blackened by the sun. After forty-seven years of solitude, now with very short, white hair, she met Zosimos, and asked him to return the following year and bury her, which he did, with the help of a friendly lion. Mary the Jewess or Prophetess was an important alchemist in the Egyptian tradition of Isis. Zosimos, writing c. AD 300, was a major successor and probably a contemporary of Mary's who developed her work. According to Saillens, the Black Virgin of Orleans was known as Ste Marie l'Egyptienne. Robert Graves calls her the patron saint of lovers and associates her with Walsingham (qv) and Compostela (qv). Her feast (2 April) is also that of the patient St Theodosia, whose statue is in the chapel of St Genevieve in St Germain-des-Prés.

There are various Pelagias who are known as penitent harlots or virgin martyrs who died to escape a fate worse than death. One, nick-named Margaret, settled on the Mount of Olives, near Bethany. She shares a feast-day, 8 October, with Thaïs, a beautiful, fourth-century Egyptian whore, about whom Anatole France wrote a novel. The most famous St Margaret, also called Marina (feast-day 20 July), was forced by her father to tend the sheep. She refused to marry the local prefect who had her imprisoned and tortured. The Devil swallowed her in the form of a dragon, but was forced to disgorge her by the cross she was wearing. Eventually she was beheaded. She is very often to be found in Black Virgin shrines, mostly in the company of St

Catherine of Alexandria, whose cultus, Attwater notes, bears some points of resemblance to hers. These two saints appeared constantly to Jeanne d'Arc, and advised her in all her heroic undertakings (though some say it was St Margaret of Scotland, not Antioch, who inspired the Maid). 'Marina' and 'Pelagia', which both mean 'of the sea', are titles of Aphrodite. The role of Marina in *Pericles, Prince of Tyre* suggests that Shakespeare may have been familiar with aspects of the esoteric, 'redeemed whore Wisdom' tradition.

St Theodata, the repentant whore of Philippi, shares a feast, 29 September, with St Michael who cast the dragon into the deep and is usually found near the Black Virgin. St Afra of Augsburg, a German repentant whore, converted by St Narcissus, shares her feast (5 August) with the Black Virgin of Rome, Our Lady of the Snows. The next day is the Transfiguration. St Euphrosyne spent thirty-eight years in a monastery disguised as a monk called Smaragdus. Lilith is Queen of Smaragd (emerald). The wisdom of Hermes Trismegistus was inscribed on emerald tablets.

ST CATHERINE OF ALEXANDRIA

St Catherine, another frequent companion of the Black Virgin, was for centuries one of the most popular saints in the calendar, whose fame was brought to the west by returning crusaders. A native of Alexandria in its third-century Gnostic apogee, royal, beautiful, rich and learned, she was, according to *Everyman's Book of Saints*, courted by the Emperor Maximian. She refused his advances and confounded a multitude of scholars assembled by him to overcome her scruples. Enraged, he had her broken on a wheel, scourged and beheaded, at which milk flowed from her veins.

It was Maximian who massacred the mutinous Theban Legion under St Maurice and resettled the Salian Franks in the Rhine-Scheldt delta. He married his daughter Fausta to Constantine in 307, the suggested year of St Catherine's martyrdom. He then led a revolt against Constantine in Gaul, which was defeated, and committed suicide at Marseilles in 310. His son Maxentius, the 'Emperor' of the story according to *The Penguin Dictionary of Saints,* was killed at the Battle of the Milvian Bridge which established Constantine and Christianity. In Butler's *Lives of the Saints,* however, Catherine's suitor is Maximinus, Caesar of the East from 305, who tried to revive paganism. It is also the name of Mary Magdalene's companion in Marseilles.

The name 'Catherine' is generally derived from the Greek root, *cathar-,* meaning pure, which may have earned her a certain popularity among Gnostic sympathisers. While she was in prison, she was fed by a dove and received a vision of Christ, which may, as in the case of her namesake from Siena, have culminated in a mystical marriage. Her body, hidden by angels, was discovered on Mount Sinai *c.*800 where the famous monastery, home of many texts from the early days of Christianity and also, reputedly, of a Black Virgin, was dedicated to her.

It is possible that the story of St Catherine's martyrdom may have been influenced by memories of the beautiful Hypatia ('highest'), subject of a historical novel of that name by Charles Kingsley. She was a philosopher and mathematician, the glory of the Neo-Platonic School of Alexandria, who was stripped naked and torn to pieces by the Christian mob.

As the patroness of young women, philosophers and scholars, Catherine symbolizes that highest feminine quality, wisdom. Is she also the tradition of the pure, Christian Gnosis of Alexandria, forced underground after the victory of the Cross at the Milvian Bridge, to re-emerge at the Crusades? In the Catherine wheel, her sign, she is one with Fortuna and de Nerval's Queen of the South. Her feast-day, 25 November, is shared by St Mercury.

ST ANNE

The cult of the mother of Our Lady was late in coming to the west and climaxed, according to Marina Warner, at the end of the fifteenth century. Her festival was not imposed by authority until 1584. In Brittany, writes Saillens, her cult generally replaces that of the Black Virgin. According to one legend, Joachim was only her first husband, the second being Cleophas, who has the same name as the father of St James and husband of

Mary who stood at the Cross with the Magdalen (John 19.25). His name is also given, in Matthew 10.3, as Alphaeus, and is that of an Arcadian river-god, the son of Thetis, who fell in love with Artemis and pursued her to Delos or Sicily. The third husband is surprisingly called Salome ('perfect'). Her body, according to Routledge's *Miniature Book of Saints*, was found in France at the time of Charlemagne by a dumb boy exclaiming, 'Here lies the body of Anne, mother of the Blessed Virgin Mary.' Her head was sent to Cologne (qv). The thirteenth-century stained glass window of her in Chartres Cathedral, next to that of Solomon, is the oldest image known to have been continuously black since its creation. Her Church in Jerusalem, built in the pure Cistercian style, was the subject of correspondence between St Bernard and Queen Mélisande. Its site by the Sheep-Gate, reputedly that of the birth-place of Mary, was the Asklepion of Jerusalem and later, under Saladin, a school of Qu'ranic wisdom. There Jesus healed a man who suffered, like Joachim, from impotence. Most of the information concerning the life of Anne and Joachim in Jerusalem derives from the apocryphal 'Protevangelium of James'. There are three characters called James in the New Testament, and it is often difficult to distinguish them in later legend. St Anne's day in the east is also that of James the Greater, Christopher and Cucufas.

ST JOHN THE BAPTIST

If, as seems likely, John was an Essene, influenced by the school of the Dead Sea Scrolls at Qumran, then he is part of a new mystical climate in Judaism, encompassing Philo's Alexandrian Therapeuts, in which the Gospel of the Kingdom was to grow and thrive. The Gnostic tradition that he represents has proved the most durable of all and still survives in Mesopotamia among the Mandaeans, also known as Nasoraeans and Christians of St John. The Merovingians, like the Nasoraeans/Nazarenes of old, never cut their hair. The Templars, too, were sometimes considered to be Christians of St John. They commemorated his feast, 24 June, which was also that of the Celtic goddess Dana with great ceremony, as the lord of the interior church. Despite the divinity of Christ, it was John who remained the master whose knowledge was the greater. Esoterically speaking, John and Jesus, born at the poles of the year, symbolise our two natures, mortal and immortal, like Castor and Pollux. The soul descends into matter in John's sign, Cancer, home of the Crib and the Asses, and journeys back to its source through Capricorn, the sign of Christ and the winter solstice. Soul and spirit, ego and self, ride the same horse of the body, but, for salvation, one must wax and the other wane. Jesus reveals that his cousin John is Elijah, who, with Moses, was also present at his Transfiguration. The feast of the beheading of John the Baptist, 29 August, is the day after that of an Ethiopian robber of the fourth century, St Moses the Black, who became a monk at Wadi Natrun in the Nile Delta. The executioner of John is, according to Saillens, regularly shown as black. We do not know what became of the head of John the Baptist after Herodias and Salome played with it and pricked its tongue. Was it the proto-Baphomet? John's name in Oc sounds the same as Janus/Dianus, to whom Robert Graves likens him. It no doubt looked both ways, back to Aries, whose sacrifice Christ fulfilled as the Lamb of God, and on to Pisces, with the symbol of the baptismal waters.

According to Rudolf Steiner, it was not only Lazarus who returned to life when Jesus said, 'Come forth.' John the Baptist also returned nineteen months after his beheading to dwell with Lazarus in one body. In his return he became one with St John the Divine, the author of the Gospel and Revelation. Thus 'he whom the Lord loved' was both John and Lazarus. The head of St Lazarus is at Andlau, close to the enlightening shrine of Mt St Odile in Alsace. Odile is the patroness of the knights who sought the Grail. Avallon also once claimed the relic and Autun still venerates its version.

CHAPTER 5
The symbolic meaning of the Black Virgin

How shall he watch at the stroke of midnight
Dove become phoenix, plumed with green and gold?
Or be caught up by jewelled talons
And haled away to a fastness of the hills
Where an unveiled woman, black as Mother Night,
Teaches him a new degree of love
And the tongues and songs of birds?

Robert Graves

There can be few people in the world interested in the poetry of myth who have not been profoundly affected by Robert Graves's inspired book *The White Goddess*. His work *Mammon and the Black Goddess* is less known. In it he states (p. 162): 'Provençal and Sicilian 'Black Virgins' are so named because they derive from an ancient tradition of Wisdom as Blackness.' He sees in her, over and above her role as ultimate inspirer of poets, the symbol of a new relationship between the sexes:

The Black Goddess is so far hardly more than a word of hope whispered among the few who have served their apprenticeship to the White Goddess. She promises a new pacific bond between men and women . . . in which the patriarchal marriage bond will fade away . . . the Black Goddess has experienced good and evil, love and hate, truth and falsehood in the person of her sisters . . . she will lead man back to that sure instinct of love which he long ago forfeited by intellectual pride.

It is paradoxical that so old an image should be seen to represent such a new and radical departure. But then it is strange, too, that the Black Virgins which have been with us so long and in such great numbers, so often hidden and rediscovered, should now for the first time become widely recognized as a separate category within the iconography of the Virgin in the west. 'We are living', wrote Jung (*The Undiscovered Self*, pp. 110f.), 'in what the Greeks called the Kairos — the right time — for a "metamorphosis of the gods", i.e. of the fundamental principles of symbols.' If this is the right time or high time for us to discover the Black Virgin, how can we know what she is trying to say to us?

We have traced her history from the great goddesses of the pre-patriarchal period, especially Inanna and her handmaiden, Lilith. One of the striking characteristics of such figures is their extraverted, uninhibited sexuality. Whether women, other than, perhaps, queens, were accustomed to dominate their lovers as Inanna with Dumuzi can only be a matter for conjecture, but if they did, it is not surprising that the pendulum should have swung to its opposite. Lilith, on the other hand, in what is admittedly a very late tradition, appears to symbolize the demand that absolute equality and a degree of independence for woman be recognized by man. Her successors in the literally patriarchal world of the Old Testament went some way towards achieving these goals, though more in the non-scriptural legends than in the Bible itself. According to these, Zipporah was able to fly off with Moses in her talons, whereas in Exodus her most notable act is to save the life of Moses, threatened by the angel of the Lord. She performs the priestly function of circumcising their elder son and blooding Moses's penis with the foreskin, perhaps as a prefiguration of the saving of the first-born of the Hebrews through the blood of the paschal lamb on the door lintels. In the story of the Queen of Sheba, although Solomon is clearly represented in the superior position, he treats his guest with great respect and near-equality, as well as giving her all that she desired.

Even the glory of the Annunciation cannot obscure the almost wholly subordinate role played by women in the New Testament. The Lilith-like Herodias and Salome have a certain seductive, manipulative power, but it is negative and destructive. Only Mary Magdalene stands out as an active, heroic figure, the first to brave official displeasure by seeking Jesus in the tomb. The name Magdala, as we have noted, means 'tower'. It is curious that, in the Litany of Loreto, the Virgin is invoked twice as 'tower' — first as 'Turris Davidica', second as 'Turris eburnea'. That the Virgin Mary, through whom, according to the genealogy of Luke, Jesus is of the line of David, should be called 'Turris Davidica', is quite appropriate. The second appellation is somewhat more surprising. Tower of Ivory is a reference to the beauty of the neck of the black Shulamite in the Song of Solomon (7.4), and in this it matches the belly of her lover (5.14). A further possible connection between Old Testament references to ivory and the history of the Black Virgin is to be found in I Kings 10.18, immediately after the departure of the Queen of Sheba, where it is given as the material of Solomon's unique bull (or ram, II Chronicles 9.21) and lion throne with its six steps.

Ivory is an arcane substance with the property of rendering flesh incorruptible. When calcined in a closed vessel, however, it yields a fine soft pigment from which the shiny ivory-black paint is made. So is what we have in the Litany two Marys, the official white and the unofficial black one? A small, further point in favour of this hypothesis can be derived from a closer look at 'Davidica' and 'eburnea'. Two towers and two cities traditionally symbolize an opposition, at least since the time of Augustine. Geographically the tower of David could only be Jerusalem, home of the Temple. Might the Greek word for ivory, *elephantinos,* yield a rival? It is generally held that there was only one Temple, but in fact a syncretistic form of Judaism flourished in the Egyptian city of Elephantiné, where there was a temple of Yahweh alongside a cult of Anath in the fifth century BC, if not earlier. Elephantiné, as a feminine adjective qualifying the understood noun *polis,* would mean city or citadel of ivory. That the Judaism there was very different from that of Ezra or Nehemiah is demonstrated by the Elephantiné papyri. We may surmise that the orthodoxy of the temple of Leontopolis at the time of the Holy Family in Egypt was equally suspect, enlightened as it would have been by the Gnostic wisdom tradition of Alexandria. It seems likely that most of the so-called wisdom literature including the Song of Solomon, the Epistle to the Hebrews and many of the finest Gnostic writings, are of Alexandrian inspiration or origin. Alexandria is also the main source of the Gnostic works linking Jesus with Mary Magdalene. According to this tradition it was through the Magdalen, rather than through Peter and the male apostles, that Jesus transmitted his secret doctrine.

It is, of course, most unlikely that the Litany of Loreto, whose use in the shrine of the Black Virgin and the Holy House is first attested in 1558 during the Council of Trent, at the height of the Counter-Reformation, should be guilty of such a heretical play on words, though the study of Greek was fashionable at the time. The early origins of the Litany of Loreto, however, date back to the twelfth century when such enigmatic associations would have been by no means improbable.

Elaine Pagels has drawn attention to the polarity that was seen to exist from the second century between Mary Magdalene and Peter. All the writings that extolled the role of Mary were ultimately excluded from the canon. In the Pistis Sophia, Mary tells Jesus of her fear of Peter: 'Peter makes me hesitate; I am afraid of him, because he hates the female race.' If we think of this polarity not in personal terms but as two traditions within Christianity, what we see are the church of Peter, catholic, orthodox, male dominated and victorious, and the rival church of Mary, Gnostic and heretical, worshipping a male/female deity and served by priests of both sexes. In the legend of the Prince of Marseilles (Chapter 4) Peter's role is that of a guide to the historical sites of Jerusalem, while Mary has the power of life and death. Triumphant Rome tried to exterminate the Church of Mary, but only succeeded in driving it underground. The rights of women were likewise repressed, though in the Celtic world they retained many of their considerable ancient freedoms. They even, according to Jean Markale, took part in the celebration of the Mass in Ireland prior to the Norman conquest. The Celtic Church long maintained many of its original practices as well as links with eastern Christianity, only yielding gradually to Rome following the Synod of Whitby (664).

It was this Celtic Christianity that re-evangelized Europe from Aachen to Lucca in the so-called Dark Ages. From the same lands came the quest for the Grail that revivified the spirituality of the twelfth century. Markale writes of the Grail quest that it is inextricable from the quest for woman (p.200). At the same period the alternative church of love resurfaced in the form of Catharism. It is resurfacing again today, partly through the interest in Gnosis that the translation of the Nag Hammadi library has aroused, partly through the new attitude towards the feminine that is one of the major characteristics of the time we live in. The main contention of this book is that the rediscovery of the Black Virgin should be seen, along with the many apparitions of the Virgin that have occurred in recent years, as a further manifestation of this same process.

Such a contention is, of course, unprovable, since all the evidence is circumstantial and associative. There is no written account of the intentions of a carver or painter of the ancient Black Virgins. Theological references to them are scant, though St Bernard took the blackness as a symbol of humility. We can only infer from this silence that, for some unknown reason, the Church was reluctant to comment officially on the phenomenon save in simplistic terms. It is, however, no longer shocking to suggest that the images represent a continuation of pagan goddess-worship and that some may have once been idols consecrated to Isis or other deities. It is also undeniable that a remarkably high proportion of Madonnas over 200 years old, that are credited with miraculous powers, are black, as are the traditional patronesses of nations, provinces and cities.

It is characteristic of Black Virgins that they resuscitate dead babies long enough to receive baptism and escape limbo, and in this they adopt a subversive posture *vis-à-vis* the rules of male-dominated theology. They are also numerous in many areas where paganism lingered or where the Cathars flourished. Quite often there is a cult of Mary Magdalene and a Black Virgin in the same place. The interest apparently shown by the Prieuré in Black Virgins, Lilith and the Queen of Sheba, and literary figures connected with them encourages the speculation that the cult of the Black Virgin has indeed links to hidden, dark secrets of the past. That past, it should be remembered, if the principal conclusion of *The Holy Blood and the Holy Grail* has any justification, includes the descent of Mérovée from the child of Jesus and Mary Magdalene.

No appeal to reason by means of such evidence as can be produced carries much weight in comparison with the appeal to the imagination that the images themselves make. The first glimpse of an ancient statue of the Black Virgin shocks and surprises. Five minutes in contemplation of her suffice to convince that one is in the presence not of some antique doll, but of a great power, the *mana* of the age-old goddess of life, death and rebirth.

For those who are able to make a leap of faith, our Black Virgin in the west has much in common symbolically with the other great goddess figures of the world. In her subterranean darkness she could be compared with the terrifying maw of death, Kali. The circles of wax dedicated to her at Moulins, Marsat and elsewhere remind us that in our end is our beginning and vice versa, of the uroboric prison of Maya and Karma, the measure of whose round-dance we must tread. She is also the ancient wisdom of Isis-Maat, the secret of eternal life that is the gold at the end of the alchemical process, as well as the initial blackness. In short, she is the spirit of evolutionary consciousness that lies hidden in matter. But evolution rejects the closed circle for the open spiral; new planets do swim into our ken, and things are not always as they have been.

The Black Virgin is a Christian phenomenon as well as a perseveration of the ancient goddesses and compensates for the one-sided conscious attitudes of the age. The Age of Pisces idealized and concretized its opposite sign, Virgo. Chastity was admired, sexuality denigrated and repressed. As the temples of the goddesses were destroyed Lilith the Leviathan languished forlornly on her ocean bed. Penitent whores became favourite cult objects, while the Virgin Mary, like Athene before her, was promoted to be the statutory female on a patriarchal board essentially hostile to woman and nature. Against the frenzied fashion for denying, defeating and transcending nature, the Black Virgin stands for the healing power of nature, the alchemical principle that the work against nature can only proceed in and through nature.

After long, slow maturing in the earth something new emerged with the buried Black Virgins in the twelfth century, something like a quantum leap in consciousness, an understanding of the symbolic significance of the relationship between the sexes. The true meaning of love had nothing to do with possessing another person, settling down, marrying and having children. Tristan tells of tragic, adulterous love, transcending the protagonists' will and giving them their journey. The troubadours came near to intuiting that the myth was the way of soul-making. But courtly

7. Marsat

love was to prove an idea whose time had not yet come and, after Dante and Petrarch, the allegorical inspiration ran out of steam, to become little more than a literary convention. The pendulum swung back and the feminine principle experienced five centuries of heavy repression.

Whatever the Black Virgin symbolizes is, to judge from her miracles, not contrary to marriage and children. At a concrete level, fertility and the home are her major concerns. They are part of the way of nature, but human nature demands more for its entelechy than the fate of beasts. The breast that nourished St Bernard fed French literature in its infancy. Roland's sword, Durendal, rightly reposes in the vulva-cleft of Rocamadour and brings fertility to brides. The poetry of the period tells of love: love of homeland ('douce France'), of companions in arms, the art of love between men and women, and the love of the Rose — not contradictory to this — that is the meaning of all love.

The Black Virgins are often associated with esoteric teaching and schools of initiation. Wisdom has always cried on the roof-tops or at the street corners, and the spirit of this world always punishes those who buy her wares. The great age of the Black Virgin is the twelfth century, but legends about her hark back to the dawn of Christianity, the dynasty of the Merovingians and the age of Charlemagne. Like the Sleepers of Ephesus, ideas go underground for a few centuries to re-emerge when times are more propitious. The idea that the meaning of life has to do with the projection and reintegration of the soul, sketched in early Gnosticism, twelfth-century poetry and in later alchemy, was not made conscious until Jung, at the same time as he was beginning his researches into Gnosticism, formulated his principle of the anima/animus.

Of the many hundred apparitions of the Virgin which have been reported as collective phenomena over the past 150 years, some, it is said, have been black. But there is now no need for her secret to be hidden, at least in the west, where sceptical indifference is a greater danger than persecution. Indeed, the secret of the Virgin must be made as widely known as possible while the conditions are relatively favourable, or the world may slip back into an age darker than those which began in the fifth or the fourteenth centuries. The one-sided patriarchal system is dying, and to cling to it is now a psychic sin. Yet it seems unlikely that a return to the matriarchate is either possible or the way ahead. In those countries of the west where starvation and tyranny are not the major problems, the great search is for meaning, and it is above all in relationships that people look for significance in their lives. Increasingly they are disappointed.

Our ancient, battered, much-loved, little-understood Black Virgins are a still-living archetypal image that lies at the heart of our civilization and has a message for us. The feminine principle is not a theory but real and it has a will of its own which we ignore at our peril. It is an independent principle and cannot be forced against its will to go anywhere or do anything without bringing retribution on the perpetrator. She brings forth, nourishes, protects, heals, receives at death and immortalizes her children who follow the way of nature. This is no different from the law of their own nature, the logos in psychology, biology, cosmology, and yet, paradoxically, it is also a work against nature. The light of nature tells us that life is a pilgrimage, a journey to the stars along the Milky Way, her hero-path, a voyage across the great water in which she is ship, rudder and guiding star. As the spirit of light in darkness she comes to break the chains of those who live in the prison of unconsciousness and restore them to their true home. In the trackless forest she is both the underground magnetism and the intuition that senses it, pointing the traveller in the right direction. She is, traditionally, the compassionate one.

If she brings forth from her treasury things both old and new, we need to be wise to what possibilities are now on offer, before it is too late. There is clearly no return to the twelfth century, the third century or the third millennium BC. Inanna, Sophia, the Holy Grail and the Church of Amor are no longer available as living realities for us today. There are signs that the goddess now requires to be worshipped in spirit and in truth through the law written in our hearts, rather than in temples built with hands. One old truth is that man and woman, though different, are equal parts of a consciously androgynous whole that is each persons's potential reality. Many people, shown photographs of the Black Virgin for the first time, comment on how masculine some of them look. Certainly Our Lady of Rocamadour is at the far end of the spectrum from the simpering examples of sacristy art that purport to represent the Virgins of Lourdes and Fatima.

Men need for the good of their souls to relate consciously to the power of the feminine or they become overwhelmed and possessed by it through their own unconsciousness. Kings, Popes and the mighty ones of the world came humbly to venerate the Black Virgins of Le Puy, Rocamadour, Montpellier and Chartres, and carried images of the powerful feminine in their hearts. Today the impression created by the infant's experience of his mother is undeniably as strong as ever, but a vision of the transpersonal Queen of Heaven, Earth and the Underworld no longer awes and inspires the imagination of adult males.

Feminists justifiably object to the sexual stereotypes by which children and indeed the whole of society are conditioned. Yet, if we have no Kali, Isis or Brigit to lighten our darkness, we have witnessed in recent times a phenomenon whose symbolic and practical importance should not be minimized. In three important nations, by the democratic will of the people, women have been raised to the position of supreme power and successfully wielded it. The authority of women is a fact of life to which the people of the west are having to accustom themselves, not just at home or in schools and hospitals, but in an ever-expanding range of occupations.

Europe had, of course, experienced female sovereigns before. There was a veritable romantic cult, by no means confined to England, that saw Queen Elizabeth as the new Astraea. She was the goddess, sister of Leto and daughter of Themis, who, when pursued by father Zeus, turned herself first into a quail, then into the island of quails, Delos, where her nephew Apollo was born. She was a goddess of the Golden Age, but when evil began to prevail on earth she was translated to the heavens, where she became the constellation Virgo. The best-selling novel in France for thirty years following its publication in 1607 was d'Urfé's *Astrée*. In Lanson's piquant phrase he 'took the arcadian pastoral and made of it a Merovingian historical novel'. Clearly the appeal of the Virgo archetype belonged to the spirit of the age.

It was, however, in Occitania, the land of the Cathars and the troubadours, that men in the Latin, Christian west first learned to honour and obey women, though not in marriage. As C. S. Lewis has shown, courtly love is adulterous and is characterized by humility and courtesy, within the context of the religion of love, though, surprisingly, he makes no reference to Catharism. Obedience to 'la Dame' and acquiescence in her rebukes had to be absolute. The phenomenon of courtly love developed at the end of the eleventh century and was formally condemned by the Church in its poetic expression by the troubadours in 1277.

C. S. Lewis proposes as the main cause of this radical new phenomenon in the history of humanity the large numbers of dependent, landless knights available in the châteaux of Languedoc to act as disciples apt to learn courtesy at the hand of the châtelaine and her ladies. This was no doubt an important factor; but surely a deeper, intrinsic attitude belonging to the time and place is at the heart of the matter, and that is the attitude of Cathars towards women and the feminine principle. One of the most remarkable and distinctive features of Catharism, which it shared with some early Gnostic groups, was that women were admitted to their priesthood of parfaits and parfaites. A celebrated example is afforded by Esclarmonde of Foix, the owner of Montségur and inspirer of its resistance, who bore eight children before, with her husband's agreement, she became a parfaite.

Cathars and troubadours, no less than Templars, exercise a powerful romantic attraction, and it is important not to idealize them. Cathar husbands at Montaillou were just as likely to beat their wives as any other peasants. There is a vein of misogyny that runs through the poetry of the troubadours from first to last, counterbalancing the extravagant service of praise accorded to the Lady. Nevertheless, Catharism and courtly love, which grew together as part of the same phenomenon, acknowledged, in theory and practice, women's freedom to take a lover. This world of incarnation was punishment enough, and the just God would not inflict further pains on those who followed the promptings of nature. To be passion's slave, however, might well entail further incarnations, and to have children would certainly prolong the time of waiting until the final purification at the end of the world. The parfaits and parfaites, who trod the path of enlightenment avoided identification with the world of matter in all its forms, but, for the simple hearers, sexual peccadilloes were not considered any worse than other deviations from that path. Indeed Cathars agreed with Plato and S Bernard that salvation began with love of bodies. Troubadours even went so far as to suggest that one must tend towards heaven through the love of women. Although both marriage and fornication were qualified as 'adultery', extra-marital union, undertaken freely, was preferable to the conjugal bond. It might even symbolize the return of the soul to its spirit after death. Nelli states categorically that Cathars and troubadours were perfectly in agreement that true love — from the soul — purified from the false love associated with marriage. The troubadour who wrote 'Flamenca' between 1250 and 1260 juxtaposes the 'Mass of Love' and the sacramental office, and made his hero serve God for the love of his lady. We are not so far in spirit from the sexual rites of Sion-Vaudémont six centuries later or from the licentious love-feasts of the Gnostics 900 years before.

Once women are free to bestow their favours and affections where they will, the whole structure of patriarchal society starts to crumble. In the long spiralling progress of the history of ideas this seems to be the point that we have once again reached. Now it is an idea whose time has come and no crusades have so far been launched by Church and State to quell it. If the Black Virgins really do carry a charge from the goddesses, perhaps, now that they have been 'found' yet again, they are whispering in our ears like the female serpent of Eden, 'You won't really die.'

Those who stress the esoteric, hidden, initiatory aspect of the Black Virgin cult are quite correct to do so in terms of the opposing orthodoxy of the Middle Ages. Now, in one sense, there are no secrets any more and wisdom cries from every paperback shelf. In another sense, everyone has to find his or her own secret, though the times may be more or less propitious for such an undertaking. The fact that so many of the Black Virgins are 'found', generally by pure serendipity, and are called Notre-Dame la Trouvée, is not without significance. The word in Oc for 'find' or 'invent' is *trobar*, from which 'troubadour', i.e. 'one who has found', is derived. But this does not by any means exhaust the possibilities of a term so rich in nuances for the practitioners of the *langue des oiseaux*. Basically, *trobar* is to express oneself in tropes, i.e. use words in a sense that differs from their normal usage. So the language of the troubadours is rich in multilingual puns, double-entendre, allusions both classical and biblical, paradox and allegory. In this language of *gay saber*, playful and tricksterish, nothing can be taken at face value. So, if a troubadour sings of his wife and his mistress, he may well be referring to the Church of Rome and Catharism. She is nagging and dangerous, this Lady, Rome, and one should not eat her meal (i.e. the Eucharist). Amor, the dark mistress, hidden underground, is the true source of light and inspiration. The most characteristic example of the hermetic *trobar clus*, elucidated by de Sède, is called 'The Death of Joana' or 'Lou Bouyé', 'the herdsman'. This song, which has become almost the national anthem of Oc, is a secret lament for the Cathar Church. Joana — Jeanne — the name given to a woman in the Cathar rituals — is found 'al pé del foc', at the foot of the fire, dead. She has gone to heaven with her goats (not sheep!). Did the pilgrims to Compostela who sang this refrain know what they were singing as they passed through the disconsolate lands? If Joana was translated to the heavens, perhaps, since the Cathars cherished astrology, we should seek her in Virgo whose wing touches the foot of the Herdsman, Boötes, where Arcturus, the bear-keeper, King Arthur, is the brightest star. On the other side of the Virgin is Crater, the cup that is both the Holy Grail and the mixing bowl in which our three natures are blended through incarnation.

The constellation Virgo, Isis to the Egyptians, is sometimes represented as a woman holding a wheatsheaf (Spica) and occasionally as a mermaid holding a child. There is, in fact, a duality at the heart of Virgo, echoing, in the age of Pisces, the contradictory nature of the two fishes. A glance at the Tarot card Justice, generally associated with the star-maiden Virgo, shows her with a sword in her right hand and a pair of scales in her left reminding us that Virgo and Libra were once one. Now, Venus ruled Libra has been sundered from Virgo, whose lord is androgynous Mercury. Balance, mercy, harmony, equilibrium have been split off from Justice, who, now, wields Spica, the spike or point, rather than Spica the ear of corn, or Triptolemus the fruit of the womb of the Eleusinian Virgin. Rákóczi writes of this card:

> To the more licentious it represented the 'virgin quality' that is gained, not by pure living, but by plunging into the abyss of sexual indulgence; here we have the exaltation of

the prostitute as a saint and the saint treated as one who is 'impure'. Hence, Gypsies often call this the Magdalene card and say that it is under the patronage of Sara, the Negress Saint of the Romany.

To the Cathar troubadour as to the psalmist it seemed as though there was little justice. The innocent were punished and the wicked flourished like the green bay-tree. These suffering righteous ones point to the unacceptable paradox at the heart of Christianity — a religion of love imposed by force. Virgo as the opposite sign to Christian Pisces, represents its beloved ideal, its bride and the reflection of the blind-spot in its soul. To Albertus Magnus it was Christ's rising sign. The literalization of the virginity of Mary, like the literalization of Eve's role as the wicked temptress of Genesis, broke the heart of Christianity and works of reparation to the Sacred Heart of Jesus and the Immaculate Heart of Mary have still not wholly healed the wound. Thus the dichotomy of the virgin and the whore, the good mother and the witch, continues to gnaw like an unresolved canker at the soul of modern man. The author of the Book of Revelation suffered severely from this split. The Great Woman of Heaven, the sign Virgo, the Holy Spirit and Mary Magdalene, brings forth a son who is to rule all nations with a rod of iron. She is at war with her neighbouring constellation of Hydra, the adversary of Hercules in his Cancer labour, associated here with the Great Whore of Babylon, who holds a golden cup 'full of abominations and filthiness of her fornication'. This may refer to the menstrual blood and semen consumed sacramentally by some Gnostic groups.

Like all true symbols, the glyph for Virgo ♍, is a meditation instrument capable of yielding many meanings. Some see in it the girdle of hymen and the promise of the immaculate conception of a Messiah. To others it is the wavy symbol of the primal waters attached to the cross of matter. Can we see folded wings, a fish-tail, the double 'M' of Mary Magdalene, the 'MR' of Maria Regina, or M followed by the healing symbol of pharmacopoeia? Pertoka interprets ♍ as the symbol of water and the Black Virgin, corresponding to the principle of differentiation. He gives it the phonetic value 'UR' ('primal' in German), which he explains as follows: (1) Waters in movement, in differentiation, the ear and the symbol of sound. (2) The idea of one thing covering another, or developing from it. (3) The sound of waves. (4) The moon in its various aspects. (5) The Hindu god Varuna, whose emblem is a fish, venerated with salt water and related to ideas of surrounding, enveloping, covering. Davidson relates it to the Hebrew letter 'Mem', signifying the feminine principle.

Astrologers confirm that the two open arches succeeded by a closed one in the sign Virgo are coiled chthonic energy held back by a locked door or closed circle from full manifestation in the phenomenal world. They see in it the untouched vagina and generative organs or the coils of the digestive tract, ruled by Virgo, where the process of refinement and differentiation occurs. Virgo is the sixth sign, at the end of the first half of the zodiac, the last of the six steps leading to personal achievement and a transition to the second circle where the individual learns to relate to the greater whole, including the transpersonal world. It thus has to do with the natural processes that are also mysteries of transformation which we experience as birth, sex and death. In Egyptian paintings the dead are swallowed by a viper to be reborn in the form of a scarab from its tail. The viper thus plays the role of the transforming alembic in alchemy. In whisky-distilling the indispensable copper condensing-pipe of Isis and Venus is known as the worm, which is also the old English word for dragon or great serpent. The wouivre (viper) is a telluric current, perhaps an underground stream, a geological fault, a vein of metal or a ley-line — a prehistoric track joining two prominent points in the landscape. It is generally invisible, but can be detected by sensitives or dowsers. It is the flow of our own life-current and the energy of the cosmos. Often a Black Virgin marks the site of a wouivre.

Virgo is not only the perpetual flux of Heraclitus but the principle that contains the flux. The containing transformer belongs to Maria Prophetissa, the alchemist, who is credited with inventing both the still and the bain-marie, whose heat, like that of the womb, is gentle and steady. In this sense Virgo is the great mother, Demeter, from whom Virgo borrows her wheat sheaf. She looks, sorrowing, for Persephone in the underworld as the Magdalen sought Jesus in the tomb, as Isis searched fo

Osiris, Freyja for Frey, Orpheus for Eurydice and Dionysus for Semele.

Sophia that is above hovers over the waters, awakening her daughter and counterpart that is below. The Virgin Mother Isis has a second major arcanum in the Tarot, Temperance, called by Sally Nichols 'the heavenly alchemist'. She is a winged figure in red, blue and gold, holding a vessel in each hand, between which a double stream of silver — or perhaps quicksilver — liquid flows. The trump signifies transformation, or light in darkness, and is connected with Aquarius, the spirit of the coming age. It comes immediately after 'Death'.

There is a third trump connected with both Venus and Aquarius, 'The Star'. Its number, 17, associated with the Prieuré and Noah's Ark, also plays a part in the story of Mary the Egyptian. Paul Huson claims that 'it hails the rebirth of Dionysus.' It comes as a ray of hope after the salutary disaster of 'The Tower Struck by Lightning', the destruction of Babel or, perhaps, the massacre of the innocents after the fall of Montségur. The Star-Woman, the first human form to appear naked in the Tarot, pours the waters of life and truth from two vessels into a river. She kneels on one knee like Jesus and Asmodeus at Rennes, and is crowned with stars like Isis and Nerval's Queen of the South. The two trees (rose and acacia?) which frame her remind us of the trees of Knowledge and Life in Eden and the water, which flows from near her womb, emphasizes the feminine source of all life on earth. But there is another source and home in the sky. The seven stars above her symbolize the planetary stages in the soul's journey. The eighth great star, at their centre, which transcends them, is either Uranus, ruler of Aquarius, or the Ogdoad, where freedom from the lower spheres may begin, the realm, to the Gnostic Ophites, of the Mother. The soul's spiritual essence is starry and falls into matter through the planetary spheres. To the Valentinians, the Ogdoad was formed from the Supreme Being, called Depth, and the First Thought, Ennoia, also named Grace or Silence. From these were born Mind, the 'Only-Begotten' and Truth. The two other syzygies completing the divine eightsome are Logos (Word) and Life, with Anthropos (Man) and Ecclesia (Church, or assembly summoned by a crier).

Lest we should seem to be straying too far from our main theme, let us recall that the Tarot is a product of that fourteenth century that saw the destruction of the Order of the Temple, the eradication of Catharism in the Languedoc, the Black Death and the Hundred Years War. It presents in symbolic form the concentrated doctrine of heretical, dualist Christianity, particularly Catharism, though it is also associated with the Gypsies and, through its 22 Trumps which correspond to the letters of the Hebrew alphabet, with Cabbalistic Judaism. In such circles, astrology was held in high esteem, and systems, like that of Joachim of Flora, which predicted the coming of the age of the Holy Spirit, were closely studied. Not for nothing is 'The Star' believed to be that which led the Magi and the Three Kings of Cologne to the manger at Bethlehem and will lead the Wise Ones again to the source of meaning and redemption. But to see Gnosticism principally in terms of divination and prognostication is to fail to understand it. When examined from the standpoint of depth psychology the account it presents of the mystery and tragedy of life is far from ridiculous. Perhaps Gnostics might prefer the term 'Height Psychology', but then 'altus' in Latin means both 'deep' and 'high'.

As it was, the stream of knowledge had to flow underground for a time. The Tarot could be presented as just a game or a relatively harmless way of fortune-telling, though the churches have always looked askance at it. In the fortress of Toursac (see Monjou) which was inhabited by Templars well after the dissolution of the Order, a Jesuit in 1687 discovered in a hiding-place a remarkable Tarot deck with portraits of contemporary figures from the fourteenth and fifteenth centuries. These included Joan of Arc, her companions-in-arms Dunois and La Hire, the alchemist pope of Avignon, John XXII and Philip van Artevelde who led the Flemings against France and captured Bruges on the Feast of the Holy Blood.

Apart from the Tarot there were two other related forms in which heretical Gnosticism continued to flourish clandestinely in the west. Astrology kept the images of the pagan gods and goddesses alive in the minds of the people and spoke, through the horoscope, of an individual path for each person as a microcosm here below reflecting the macrocosm above. Alchemy, in its essence the art of psychic transformation, the 'yoga of

Gnosticism' as Quispel has called it, was recognized by Jung as the chief precursor of modern depth psychology. Of secret societies which exist alongside official religion and have generally been hostile to it, two relevant to our theme are the Freemasons, founded in the twelfth century under the patronage of St John the Baptist, and the Rosicrucians. Both have been associated by the authors of *The Holy Blood and the Holy Grail* with the Prieuré.

The underground stream, called by Coleridge Alph, is Alphaeus, 'the leprous one', which disappears at Arcadia to rise again in Sicily as the Fountain of Arethusa ('the waterer'), a goddess of springs, like Briccia, and one of the four Hesperides who form Venus, the evening star. Alphaeus, as we have seen, is also father of the Apostle James the Less, or Shorter, of whom little is known other than his feast-day, 1 May which is also that of Belen, Venus, Siegmund the Arian, Joseph the Workman and, formerly, Amadour. He is confused in Butler's *Lives of the Saints* with 'the best-known of all the apostles, son of Zebedee and a kinsman of Our Lord', James of Compostela. More commonly he is identified with James the Just, the brother of the Lord, one of the characters in the Gnostic writings whom Jesus kissed on the mouth. In the Gnostic Gospel of Thomas a remarkable claim is made for him: 'The disciples said to Jesus, "We know that you will depart from us. Who is to be our leader?" Jesus said to them, "Wherever you are, you are to go to James the righteous, for whose sake heaven and earth came into being."' It is likely that he represented the original Judaeo-Christian Gnostic teaching, which was also associated with Mary Magdalene, and which saw itself as betrayed by the later orthodox Catholicism that claimed to be the Church of Peter and Paul. The Gnostic saint lives on in England in 'The Court of St James', named after a twelfth-century leper hospital dedicated to him.

Is the Black Virgin a symbol of the hidden Church and of the underground stream? The Laffont *Dictionnaire des Symboles* defines virginity as the unmanifest and unrevealed. Blackness redoubles this significance. Concerning the symbolism of Black Virgins the *Dictionary* sees them as the virgin earth, not yet fecundated, thus emphasizing the passive quality of virginity. They are the womb of the earth or of the soul like those goddesses that are also sometimes shown as black — Isis,

Athene, Demeter, Cybele and Aphrodite. The *Everyman Dictionary of Non-Classical Mythology* simply sees in Black Virgins the continuation of the cult of Isis, as Christianity took over her chapels and her images. It adds: 'In . . . Les Saintes Maries de la Mer, Isis has been demoted to the rank of a serving-maid with the name of Sara, in which capacity she is still the divinity of the gypsies.' So the Great Goddess is now unmanifest, save as mother of the outcast gypsies.

Depth psychology has shown that the unmanifest has two levels, the personal unconscious and the collective unconscious. The unconscious, however, is not completely dark. The alchemists observed a stage in the opus which they called variously the leprosy of the metals or the blessed greenness. After an individual has poured his or her energies outwards into the world there may come a point at which the thirst for a new source of meaning begins to make itself felt. Virgo is the end of the first half of life that belongs to the conscious ego. John the Baptists's task, undertaken in Cancer (24 June), where souls come into incarnation, ends its first phase in Virgo with the sacrifice of his head (29 August). Then he is at one with the leper Lazarus and Elijah the green with his fiery soul-chariot, Elijah who in the Middle Ages became Helyas the Artist, the master of alchemy. The great work of the second half of life must be based on the Virgoan virtue of discrimination between the way of the world and one's own inner truth.

The Black Virgin reminds us that we have an alternative, and that not all roads lead to Rome. Isis the alchemist, in whose myth are contained all the elements of the art, is still with us. The real name of Egypt and alchemy both derive from Khem, 'black earth'. The Greek *chemia* means 'transmutation' and has been confused with *chumeia*, a mingling and *chuma*, 'that which is poured'. Not only are we, in the Gnostic view, a mixture of three elements — body, soul and spirit, as different as the salt, sulphur and mercury from which the alchemists prayed a fourth would emerge, we are also the result of the blended genes of all our ancestors and of the disparate factors in our conditioning that have formed our personalities. Underneath all our conditioning, hidden in the crypt of our being, near the waters of life, the Black Virgin is enthroned with her Child, the dark latency of our own essential nature, that which we were always meant to be.

Sometimes she comes to us in dreams and visions, in sickness cured, in rescue from catastrophe and in chance encounters with the numinous. The legends of her shrines are full of such experience.

Historically, the Black Virgin cult seems to point in the direction of two alternatives in particular. One, the alternative Church of Mary Magdalene, James, Zacchaeus, Gnosticism, Cathars, Templars and alchemists, we have circumambulated many times, peering at it from different angles. It contains much of the wisdom of the old religions as well as certain new phenomena that reached consciousness in the twelfth century, such as the Holy Grail and courtly love. If guilt by association is an admissible form of evidence — and it is all we have — then the Black Virgin can by no means be absolved of associating with some strange companions belonging to the alternative Church. The problem of the once and future king in exile, posed by the Prieuré de Sion, presents a different problem which has not yet been solved, but it may be significant that their mother-house in Jerusalem was adjacent to Bethany.

Books about Black Virgins prior to 1982 did not concern themselves with the Prieuré de Sion or the fortunes of the Merovingian dynasty, and it was not my original intention to break with this precedent. *The Holy Blood and the Holy Grail* made no mention of Black Virgins, but one of the authors alerted me to a possible correlation between them and the Prieuré. Then I read *Rennes-le-Château* in which Brétigny and Deloux refer to the Black Virgins of Blois, Limoux, Marseilles, Goult-Lumières and Sion-Vaudémont in the context of the Prieuré and its history. As my researches continued, it became increasingly obvious that the cult of the Black Virgin and the history of the Merovingian blood-line were inextricably linked.

The significance of this link is as mysterious as everything else to do with the Prieuré. That they should work for the restoration of the Merovingian dynasty, possibly at the head of a united Europe, is comprehensible, if somewhat eccentric. If they believe, and the point is left unclear in *The Holy Blood and the Holy Grail*, that the blood-line pretender is a descendant of Mary Magdalene, then her shrines, of which there are many in France, would seem to offer an appropriate symbol and rallying-point for the order without any need to symbolize her as the

Black Virgin. That they may also be interested in pursuing their aims by occult means should afford no surprise. Hitler's new order depended, he is reputed to have believed, on the magical power of the Jewish Spear of Destiny from the Hofburg in Vienna. The Compagnie du Saint Sacrement and the Rosicrucians seem to have been inspired by political as well as spiritual goals. The role of the Black Virgin, if any, in the furtherance of these ends is, however, far from clear, unless we conclude that the Prieuré chooses to see in her the alternative Mary, the Magdalen, and all she stands for.

It is not only Christianity that is divided into two Churches, with the hidden one sometimes represented as the synagogue. Mary may stand for something else which we have not yet considered and that is heretical Judaism. It is here that the origins of Gnosticism as a historical phenomenon are to be found, and it is here that Jew and Christian are at one. Always in the background of our story is the hidden history of Judaism, with its back-sliding tendencies in the direction of the Goddess. The Merovingians claim descent from Noah and from the heretical, outcast tribe of Benjamin — sodomite sons of Belial — who emigrated to Arcadia and thence, like Alphaeus, to Sicily. It then formed the sacred dance sodality of the Salians in Rome. The Salians were also the priestly tribe of the Ligurian peoples, Provençal worshippers of the Goddess, whose descendants Mary Magdalene no doubt encountered. Many interesting references are to be found in *The Holy Blood and the Holy Grail* to the presence of Jews in Languedoc and Roussillon, where the words Goth and Jew were confused and frequently interchangeable. Dagobert's Visigothic father-in-law's sister married into a family called Lévi, one of whom no doubt brought the young Sigebert to Rennes-le-Château. Rennes itself has for its coat of arms the six-pointed star of David or seal of Solomon, and ancient Jewish inscriptions have been found in the area. The blood-line, it is claimed, continued through the rulers of the Jewish principality based on Visigothic Septimania with its capital of Narbonne, whose boundaries correspond to the later projected Templar realm north and south of the Pyrenees.

In the north, too, the Jewish connection is all-pervasive. The nearest village to Stenay is Baalon. According to de Sède, this commemorates the Syrian god Baal, whose worship Solomon reintroduced to Israel by dedicating a temple to him on the Mount of Olives, near Bethany. Stenay probably owes its name to Baal. It was his devouring Saturn/Moloch aspect to which children were sacrificed, especially at Yule-tide. The Church of St Dagobert was built on the site of the temple of Saturn/Moloch. The nearest Black Virgin to Stenay is at Avioth, a Hebrew word meaning 'ancestors', where children were also sacrificed. Shortly before the establishment of the Jewish/Merovingian principality of Narbonne an event of major importance occurred at the opposite end of Europe. In 740 the powerful empire of the Kazars adopted Judaism as its state religion under the guidance of Spanish Jews. Arthur Koestler argues that it is these Kazars who formed the great Jewish population of eastern Europe and thus constitute the majority of Jews, the Ashkenazim, throughout the world. He suggests that the German word for heretic, *Ketzer,* is derived from Kazar, and produces evidence that Yiddish is derived from Crimean Gothic. The emigration route from the east taken by the Kazars is strikingly similar to that taken by the Goths and Sicambrian Franks centuries before, though some Kazar incursions in eastern Europe dated from the mid-fifth century. The heretical Karaite Jews, whose name probably means 'dark', and who spend the sabbath in darkness, are aware of these secrets and have links to both eastern and western Jewry.

The old Jewish communities which had existed from the days of the Roman Empire along the Rhine and in France were, after much suffering, destroyed or exiled during the thirteenth and fourteenth centuries. Philippe le Bel confiscated their goods and expelled them on the feast of Mary Magdalene, 1306, a year before he arrested the Templars. The expulsion of the Jews from Spain and Portugal in 1492 and 1497, where they had formed an important part of the population, created vast numbers of forcibly converted Jews, constantly suspected of heresy by the Inquisition. These Jews either stayed where they were as part of the hidden Church, or spread their beliefs to other parts of Europe. The great wave of Jewish emigration from Poland and Russia to the west did not begin until 1648. It seems quite possible, however, that the links between western Jews and eastern Kazar/Jews, forged in the eighth century, were not totally broken in the intervening millennium and that those claiming descent from the Kings of Israel in France would have been aware of this 'heretical' Jewish secret. The Merovingians were accused of being *rois fainéants*, that is sacred rulers who did not occupy themselves with the day-to-day work of government, which was left to the Mayors of the Palace, who eventually usurped their throne. It is remarkable that a similar division of divine and secular power prevailed among the Kazars in the tenth century, a division symbolized by the king and queen of the chess-board. It seems that the passive role of the Kagan, or sacred king, dates from after the conversion of the Kazar Empire to Judaism. The idea of two rulers is not a new one to Judaism though Jewish kings were far from *rois fainéants*. At Qumran, however, in the Essene Jewish community that produced the Dead Sea Scrolls and may have had a distant influence on the heretical Nestorian Church, there was a strong tradition of two Messiahs, priestly and secular. John the Baptist and James the Just, both members of the priesthood and both influenced by the Essene tradition of Qumran, were considered to be the Priestly Messiah or Teacher. Jesus, on the other hand, was claimed to be the Messiah, son of David. The only person who called him by this title was blind Bartimeus ('son of the honoured one' — Timaeus was Plato's Pythagorean interlocutor). He was healed by Jesus immediately prior to the Zacchaeus episode, just after James and John have asked Jesus for places on his right and left hand when he enters into glory. Perhaps Bartimeus is the same person as Cedonius, the companion of Mary Magdalene on the voyage to France. Nathaniel/Bartholomew who also hails Jesus as King of Israel, was flayed in Armenia like St Blaise, and, like St James, is associated with St Philip. When Pantaenus (*c.*180), founder of the Catechetical School of Alexandria, visited India he was told Bartholomew had preached the Gospel there.

Some of the Church fathers state that James was both High Priest and of the line of David. Like the Merovingian kings, he never cut his hair. The Teacher of Righteousness, Zadok, whose name means 'just' or 'righteous', has been associated with John the Baptist. According to the 'Clementine Recognitions' two of John's closest disciples, who succeeded him as leaders of the Zadokites, were Simon Magus, 'father of all heresies', and Dositheus, a Samaritan heretic whose disciples held that he had not really died. According to other accounts, the Dositheans were a sect dating back to Maccabaean times. The Maccabaeans proved a great disappointment to the righteous, who withdrew to desert caves like Qumran. It is perhaps significant in this connection that in Lyons, hotbed of second-century Gnosticism, the Church of the Maccabees, near the present church of the Black Virgin on the plateau of Sarra, was rededicated to St Just, who had withdrawn to the Egyptian desert. Two other people referred to as 'just' in the New Testament are Joseph of Arimathea who possessed the Grail and Joseph Barsabbas ('son of man, or Sheba'?), defeated in the election to the Twelve by Matthias. A saint called Dositheus traditionally brought the Virgin of St Luke to Valvanera, valley of Venus.

Disappointed apocalypticism is commonly transmuted into mysticism, and that of Qumran seems to have been no exception to this principle. At the end of a millennium, however, or of a platonic great year, and when danger threatens, people long once more for the coming of the Messiah, Saviour or once and future king. As we approach the year 2000 and the age of Aquarius, amid prophecies of impending nuclear doom, Messianic hopes are once more stirring in many hearts, including, perhaps, those of the Prieuré. After the last battle the Grand Monarque will arise and reign from Avignon, ancient city of Cathars and Popes, watched over by a Black Virgin. This is foretold by Nostradamus, Merovingian propagandist as well as prophet, descendant of converted Jews who adopted a masculine form of Our Lady as their name. Nostradamus learned his wisdom at Montpellier and Orval, before settling at Salons, the city of the Salians. The Grand Monarque, of 'Trojan blood and Germanic heart' who is also 'King of Blois' and 'Belgic', is presumably of the Merovingian blood-line. He will restore the Church 'to pristine pre-eminence', though Rome and the Barque of St Peter will be destroyed. As all this is scheduled to happen before 1999, when Nostradamus predicts what seems to be the end of the world, it is no wonder that a sense of urgency should have motivated the Prieuré, after so many centuries of secrecy, to reveal itself and its aims to the world. Meantime let us hope that the Virgin turns towards us her 'most merciful face of night' as we recall that, to the Sufis, blackness is the final stage of the journey of the soul towards beatitude.

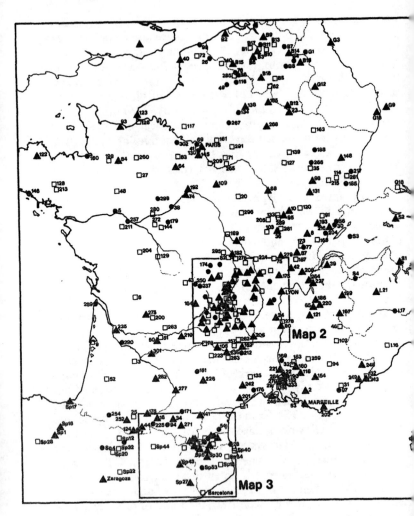

Map No. 1

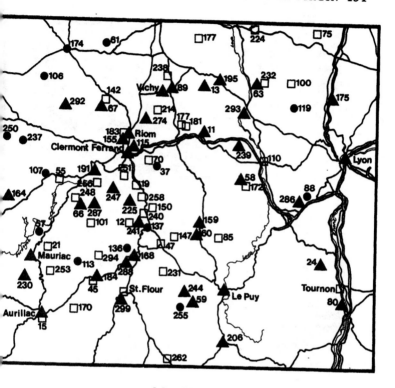

Map No. 2

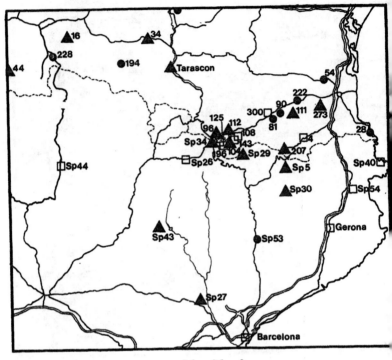

Map No. 3

Bibliography

Adams, H., *Mont-Saint-Michel and Chartres*, London, 1913, 1980.

Alexander, W. L., *The Ancient British Church*, London, 1889.

Algermissen, K., *Lexikon der Marienkunde*, Regensburg, 1957.

Allegro, J. M., *The Sacred Mushroom and the Cross*, London, 1973.

Alliès, A.-P., *Pézenas une ville d'États*, Montpellier, 1951.

Alvárez de la Braña, R., 'Palencia monumental y la Virgen de Husillos', *Boletín de la Sociedad Castellana de Excursiones*, año 1, no. 4, 1903.

Apuleius, *The Golden Ass*, trans. Robert Graves, London, 1951.

Aradi, Z., *Shrines to Our Lady*, New York, 1954.

Arès, J.d', 'Les vierges noires en France', *Atlantis*, no. 266, pp.123-32, 1972.

Arès, J. d'., 'A propos des vierges noires', *Atlantis*, no. 266, pp. 184–92, 1972.

Ashe, G., *The Virgin*, London, 1976.

Attwater, D., *The Penguin Dictionary of Saints*, Harmondsworth, 1965.

Auden, W. H. and Taylor, P. B. (trans.), *The Elder Edda*, London, 1969.

Bac, H., 'La vierge noire des Atlantes', *Atlantis*, no. 266, pp.147-55, 1972.

Bader, K., *Pfarr- und Wallfahrtskirche Leutershausen*, Ottobeuren, 1977.

Baedeker, K., *Northern Italy*, London, 1913.

Baigent, M. and Leigh, R., 'Virgins with a pagan past', *The Unexplained*, no. 4, pp.61-5, 1980.

Baigent, M. and Leigh, R., 'The goddess behind the mask', *The Unexplained*, no. 6, pp.114-17, 1980.

Baigent, M. and Leigh. R., 'Guardians of the living earth', *The Unexplained*, no. 8, pp. 154–7, 1980.

Baigent, M. Leigh, R. and Lincoln, H., *The Holy Blood and the Holy Grail*, London, 1982.

Balme, P. and Crégut, R., *La Basilique Notre-Dame du Port*, Clermont-Ferrand, 1971.

Bardy, B., *Les Légendes du Gévaudan*, Mende, 1979.

Barrès, M. *La Colline inspirée*, Paris, 1913.

Bauer, W., *Orthodoxy and Heresy in Earliest Christianity*, London, 1934, 1972.

Beaufrère, A., *Notre-Dame du Château à St Christophe*, Aurillac, undated.

Begg, E., 'Gnosis and the single vision', in M. Tuby (ed.), *In the Wake of Jung*, London, 1983.

Begg, E., *Myth and Today's Consciousness*, London, 1984.

Beicht, W., *Maria Himmelfahrt Ludwigshafen-Oggersheim*, Ludwigshafen, 1977.

Belot, V., *La France des pélérinages*, Verviers, 1976.

Benoit, P., *L'Atlantide*, Paris, 1920, 1974.

Berland, J., 'Meymac et son abbaye', *Bulletin de la Société des Lettres, Sciences et Arts de la Corrèze*, pp.5-77, 1975.

Bernard, J.-L., *Histoire secrète de Lyon et du Lyonnais*, Paris, 1977.

Bertrand, M., *Histoire secrète de la Provence*, Paris, 1978.

Bible. Various translations.

Blanc, P., *La Charité à Espalion*, Rodez, 1973.

Blanquart, H., 'La basilique hermétique de Guingamp', *Atlantis*, no. 253, pp.402-30, November 1961.

Bodeson, J., *Verviers Notre-Dame des Récollets*, Liège, 1972.

Bordenove, G., *Histoire secrète de Paris*, Paris, 1980.

Bouvet, R., *Notre-Dame de l'Aumône*, Rumilly, 1982.

Bouvier-Ajam, M., *Dagobert*, Paris, 1980.

Boymann, G. and O., *The Basilica at Kevelaer*, Munich, 1978.

Bradley, M., *The Mists of Avalon*, London, 1984.

Brétigny, J., 'Les vierges noires et le mystère de Rennes-le-Château', *Nostra*, March 1983.

Brétigny, J. and Deloux, J.-P., *Rennes-le-Château capitale secrète de l'histoire de France*, Paris, 1982.

Briffault, R., *The Mothers*, New York, 1977 (abridged), 1927.

Bril, J., *Lilith ou la mère obscure*, Paris, 1981.

Brion, M., *Frédéric II de Hohenstaufen*, Paris, 1978.

Bridge, W., *The Gods of the Egyptians*, London, 1904.

Buenner, D., *Notre-Dame de la Mer et les Saintes-Maries*, Lyons, undated.

Buisson, P., *La Vierge Noire du Charmaix*, Modane, 1984.

Burri, M., *Germanische Mythologie zwischen Verdrängung und Verfälschung*, Zürich, 1982.

Butler, A. (ed. Kelly, B.), *The Lives of the Fathers, Martyrs and Other Principal Saints*, 5 vols, London, 1959.

Campbell, J., *The Masks of God*, New York, 1964.

Campbell, J. (ed.), *The Mystic Vision*, Eranos Yearbooks, vol. 6, London, 1969.

Canseliet, E., 'Notre-Dame de dessous-terre', *Atlantis*, no. 266, pp.155-63, 1972.

Carny, L., 'Les vièrges noires en France', *Atlantis*, no. 206, pp. 163-8, 1962.

Cauvin, A. *Découvrir la France Cathare*, Verviers, 1974.

Cazes, A., *Tuir*, Prades, undated.

Cazes, A., *Le Roussillon sacré*, Prades, 1977.

Cazes, A., *Prats-de-Molló et sa région*, Prades, 1978.

Chabrillat, R., *Thuret son eglise d'initiés son saint*, Clermont-Ferrand, 1979.

Chagny, A., *Notre-Dame de la Garde*, Marseilles, 1949.

Champagnac, J.-B., *Dictionnaire des pélérinages*, Paris, 1850.

Champion, P., *Le Roi Louis XI*, Paris, 1936.

Charles, R. H. (trans.), *The Book of Enoch*, London, 1912.

Charpentier, J., *L'Ordre des Templiers*, Paris, 1977.

Charpentier, L., *Les Mystères templiers*, Paris, 1967.

Charpentier, L., *Les Jacques et le mystère de Compostelle*, Paris, 1971.

Charpentier, L., *The Mysteries of Chartres Cathedral*, London, 1972.

Chartuni, M., *Nossa Senhora de Aparecida*, São Paolo, undated.

Chevalier, J. and Gheerbrant, A., *Dictionnaire des symboles*, Paris, 1969.

Chevallier, B. and Goulay, B., *Je vous salue Marie*, Paris, 1981.

Cirlot, J., *A Dictionary of Symbols*, London, 1962.

Clarke, C., *Everyman's Book of Saints*, London, 1914, 1956.

Coadic, J.-B., *Notre-Dame de Bon Secours de Guingamp*, Guingamp, 1933.

Cohn, N., *Europe's Inner Demons*, London, 1975.

Colin-Simard, A., *Les Apparitions de la Vierge*, Paris, 1981.

Colquhoun, H., *Our Descent from Israel*, Glasgow, 1931.

Colson, J., *Sion-Vaudémont ou la colline inspirée*, Paris, 1978.

Comte, L., *The Cathedral of Le Puy and its Environs*, Colmar, 1978.

Cooper, J., *An Illustrated Encyclopaedia of Traditional Symbols*, London, 1978.

Croix, M., 'La vierge de Châtillon-sur-Seine dite du miracle de la lactation' *Aesculape*, no. 1, January 1932.

Cross, F. L. (ed.), *The Oxford Dictionary of the Christian Church*, London, 1958.

Dailliez, L., *La France des Templiers*, Verviers, 1974.

Daniel-Rops, H., *The Church in the Dark Ages*, London, 1959.

Darcy, G. and Angebert, M., *Histoire secrète de la Bourgogne*, Paris, 1978.

Davidson, H. R. Ellis, *Gods and Myths of Northern Europe*, Harmondsworth, 1964.

Davidson, R., *Astrology*, London, 1963.

Dawson, L., *A Book of the Saints*, London, undated.

Delaporte, Y., *Les trois Notre-Dame de la cathédrale de Chartres*, Paris, 1965.

Delarue, L., *Notre-Dame de Lumières*, Lyons, 1973.

Delsante, U., *Collecchio: Strutture Rurale e Vita Contadine*, Parma, 1982.

Denis, N. and Boulet, R., *Romée ou le pélérin moderne à Rome*, Paris, 1935.

Dereine, G., *La Légende de Notre-Dame de Walcourt*, Namur, 1975.

Devore, N., *Encyclopaedia of Astrology*, New York, 1947.

Drochon, J. E., *Histoire illustrée des pélérinages français de la Très Sainte Vierge*, Paris, 1890.

Duchaussoy, J., 'Vierges cosmiques et vierges noires', *Atlantis*, no. 226, pp.164-8, 1972.

Duhoureau, B., *Guide des Pyrénées mystérieuses*, Paris, 1973.

Dumas, F., *Histoire secrète de la Lorraine*, Paris, 1979.

Dumoulin, J. and Pycke, J., *La Cathédrale Notre-Dame de Tournai*, Tournai, 1980.

Dupuy-Pacherand, F., 'Les vierges noires et les déesses pré-chrétiennes', *Atlantis*, no. 205, November, 1961.

Dupuy-Pacherand, F., 'Du symbolisme cosmique aux vierges noires', *Atlantis* no. 266, pp.133-46, 1972.

Durand-Lefèbvre, M., *Etude sur l'origine des Vierges Noires*, Paris, 1937.

Eales, S., *St Bernard*, London, 1890.

Escot, J., *Fourvière à travers les siècles*, Lyons, 1954.

Fanthorpe, P. and L., *The Holy Grail Revealed*, North Hollywood, 1982.

Faux, A., *Notre-Dame du Puy*, Le Puy, 1979.

Fernández y Sánchez, P., *Mariología Extremeña*, awaiting publication.

Fisher, C., *Walsingham Lives On*, London, 1979.

Fleury, R de, *La Sainte Vierge*, Paris, 1878.

Foatelli, N., 'La vierge noire de Paris Notre-Dame-de-Bonne-Délivrance', *Atlantis*, no. 266, pp.180-3, 1972.

Forsyth, I., *The Throne of Wisdom*, Princeton, 1972.

Foucher, E., *Notre-Dame de la Délivrande*, La Délivrande, 1983.

France, A., *Thaïs*, Paris, 1890.

France, A., *La Rôtisserie de la Reine Pédauque*, Paris, 1893.

Franz, M.-L. von, *Aurora Consurgens*, London, 1966.

Franz, M.-L. von, *Apuleius' Golden Ass*, New York, 1970.

Franz, M.-L. von, *C.G. Jung: His Myth in Our Time*, London, 1975.

Franz, M.-L. von, *Alchemy*, Toronto, 1980.

Fraser, J., *The Golden Bough*, 1922.

Fröhlich, H., *Ein Bildnis der Schwarzen Muttergottes von Brünn in Aachen*, Mönchengladbach, 1967.

Fsadni, M., *Our Lady of the Grotto*, Rabat, 1980.

Fulcanelli, *Le Mystère des cathédrales*, London, 1971.

Furneaux, R., *The Other Side of the Story*, London, 1971.

Gage, M., *Woman, Church and State*, Watertown, 1893, 1980.

Gascuel, E., *Notre-Dame de la Brune*, Roumégoux, 1958.

Gilardoni, V., *I Monumenti d'Arte e di Storia del Canton Ticino*, Basle, 1979.

Gordon, P., *Les Vierges Noires*, Essais, Paris, 1983.

Gordon, P., *Les Fêtes à travers les ages*, Paris, 1983.

Gostling, F., *Auvergne and its People*, London, 1911.

Graves, R., *The Greek Myths*, Harmondsworth, 1955.

Graves, R., *The White Goddess*, London, 1961.

Graves, R., *Mammon and the Black Goddess*, London, 1964.

Graves, R. and Patai, R., *Hebrew Myths*, London, 1964.

Grigson, G., *The Goddess of Love*, London, 1976.

Groningen, G. van, *First Century Gnosticism*, Leiden, 1967.

Guirand, F. (ed.), *New Larousse Encyclopedia of Mythology*, London, 1959.

Guirdham, A., *The Cathars and Reincarnation*, London, 1970.

Gumppenberg, G., *Atlas Marianus*, 1657-9.

Gumppenberg, M. von, *Unsere Königin*, Munich, 1955.

Gustafson, F. R., 'The Black Madonna of Einsiedeln: A Psychological Perspective', Diploma Thesis, C. G. Jung Institute, Zürich, 1973.

Halevi, Z. ben S., *Tree of Life*, London, 1972.

Hall, N., *The Moon and the Virgin*, London, 1980.

Hamlyn, P., *Egyptian Mythology*, London, 1965.

Hamon, A., *Notre-Dame de France*, Paris, 1861.

Harding, E., *Women's Mysteries*, New York, 1955.

Harrison, J., *Themis*, London, 1911, 1977.

Helmbold, A., *The Nag Hammadi Gnostic Texts and the Bible*, Grand Rapids, 1967.

Herolt, J. (ed.), Power, E., *Miracles of the Blessed Virgin Mary*, London, 1928.

Hillman, J. (ed.), *Facing the Gods*, Dallas, 1980.

Hurwitz, S., *Lilith die Erste Eva*, Zürich, 1980.

Huson, P., *The Devil's Picture Book*, London, 1972.

Hutin, S., *Les Prophéties de Nostradamus*, Paris, 1972.

Huynen, J., *L'Enigme des Vierges Noires*, Paris, 1972.

Huysmans, J.-K., *Là-Bas*, Paris, 1908.

Huysmans, J.-K., *La Cathédrale*, Paris, 1908, 1955.

Jalenques, L., *Salers*, Clermont-Ferrand, 1970.

James, B., *Saint Bernard of Clairvaux*, London, 1957.

James, M. R., *The Apocryphal New Testament*, London, 1924, 1953.
Jean, R., *Nerval*, Paris, 1964.
Jonas, H., *The Gnostic Religion*, Boston, 1963.
Josy-Roland, F., *Notre-Dame de Walcourt*, Walcourt, 1972.
Josy-Roland, F., *La Basilique Notre Dame à Walcourt*, Walcourt, 1979.
Jung, C. G., *Psychology and Alchemy* (Collected Works, vol. 12), London, 1953.
Jung, C. G., *The Undiscovered Self*, London, 1958.
Jung, C. G., *Psychology and Religion: West and East* (Collected Works, vol. 11), London, 1958.
Jung, C. G., *Aion* (Collected works, vol. 9, part 2), London, 1959.
Jung, C. G., *Mysterium Coniunctionis* (Collected Works, vol. 14), London, 1963.
Jung, C. G., *Civilization in Transition* (Collected Works, vol. 10), London, 1964.
Jung, C. G., *Two Essays on Analytical Psychology* (Collected Works, vol 7), London, 1966.
Jung, C. G., *Symbols of Transformation* (Collected Works, vol. 5), London, 1967.
Jung, C. G., *Alchemical Studies* (Collected Works, vol. 13), London, 1967.
Jung, E. and Franz, M.-L. von, *The Grail Legend*, London, 1971.
Kerenyi, K., *The Heroes of the Greeks*, London, 1959.
Kerenyi, K., *The Gods of the Greeks*, London, 1961.
Kerenyi, K., *Hermes Guide of Souls*, Zürich, 1976.
Kerenyi, K., *Goddesses of Sun and Moon*, Dallas, 1979.
Kininmouth, C., *Traveller's Guide to Sicily*, London, 1965.
Klossowkski de Rola, S., *The Secret Art of Alchemy*, London, 1973.
Kluger, Schärf R., *Psyche and Bible*, Zürich, 1974.
Koestler, A., *The Thirteenth Tribe*, London, 1976.
Küppers, L., *Das Essener Münster*, Essen, 1963.
Lacordaire, H., *Saint Mary Magdalen*, London, 1880.
Lanson, G., *Histoire de la littérature française*, Paris, 1894.
Lauras-Pourrat, A., *Guide de l'Auvergne Mystérieuse*, Paris, 1976.
Layard, J., *A Celtic Quest*, Zürich, 1975.
Lechner, M., *Schön Schwarz bin ich: zur Ikonographie der Schwarzen Madonnen der Barockzeit*, Heimat-an-Rot w. Inn, 1971.
Legros, J., *Le Mont Sainte-Odile: Une énigme*, Paris, 1974.
Le Roy Ladurie, E., *Montaillou*, London, 1978.
Lespinasse, J., *Chroniques du Brivadois*, Brioude, 1965.
Lewis, C. S., *The Allegory of Love*, Oxford, 1936.
Lubicz, I. S. de. *Her-Bak Disciple*, Paris, 1956.
Macadam, A. (ed.), *Northern Italy*, Blue Guide, 1924, 1978.
MacDonald, G., *Lilith*, London, 1895, 1969.

MacGowan, K., *Our Lady of Dublin*, Dublin, 1970.

Magnusson, M., *Hammer of the North*, London, 1976.

Marie, F., *La Résurrection du Grand Cocu*, Paris, 1981.

Markale, J., *Women of the Celts*, London, 1975.

Martinet, S., *Laon, ancienne capitale de la France*, Laon, 1966.

Masson, J.-R. (ed.), *Guide du Val de Loire mystérieux*, Paris, 1980.

Matthews, J., *The Grail*, London, 1981.

Mead, G. R. S., *Fragments of a Faith Forgotten*, London 1900.

Michelin, *The Green Guides*.

Michell, J., *The Earth Spirit*, London, 1975.

Miller, D. L., *The New Polytheism*, Dallas, 1981.

Montaigu, H., *Histoire secrète de l'Aquitaine*, Paris, 1979.

Moreau, M., 'Origine des vierges noires', *Atlantis*, no. 205, November 1961.

Moreau, M., 'Les cultes de lumière, la déesse noire et la source', *Atlantis*, no. 206, pp. 147–61, January 1962.

Moritz-Bart, L., *Notre-Dame des Dunes et sa petite chapelle de Dunkerque*, Dunkirk, 1977.

Moss, L. and Cappannari, S., 'In Quest of the Black Virgin: She is Black because She is Black', in *Mother Worship*, ed. Preston, J., Chapel Hill, 1982.

Mylonas, G., *Eleusis and the Eleusinian Mysteries*, Princeton, 1961.

Nancray, P., 'Les déesses noires venues d'orient', *Nostra*, 31 March 1983.

Nelli, R., *Le Phénomène Cathare*, Toulouse, 1964.

Nelli, R., *L'Érotique des Troubadours*, Paris, 1974.

Neumann, E., *The Great Mother*, Princeton, 1963.

Nichols, S., *Jung and the Tarot*, New York, 1980.

Nicoll, M., *The New Man*, London, 1950.

Nicoll, M., *The Mark*, London, 1954.

Noguera i Massa, A., *Les Marededéus romaniques de les terres gironines*, Barcelona, 1977.

Nutt, A., *Studies on the Legend of the Holy Grail*, London, 1888.

Oken, A., *Complete Astrology*, New York, 1980.

Oldenbourg, Z., *Le Bûcher de Montségur*, Paris, 1959.

Oliver, G., *Breve Historia del Santuario y Colegio de Nuestra Señora de Lluch*, Palma, 1976.

Oursel, R., *Le Procès des Templiers*, Paris, 1955.

Ousset, P., *Notre-Dame de Miège-Coste à Aspet*, Comminges, 1959.

Pagels, E., *The Gnostic Gospels*, London, 1980.

Parker, D., and J., *The Compleat Astrologer*, London, 1971.

Perera, S. B., *Descent to the Goddess*, Toronto, 1981.

Pernoud, R., *Vie et mort de Jeanne d'Arc*, Paris, 1953.

Pernoud, R., *Les Hommes de la Croisade*, Paris, 1982.

Pertoka, A., *Recherches sur le symbolisme des Vierges Noires*, Zürich, 1974.

Peyrard, J., *Histoire secrète de l'Auvergne*, Paris, 1981.

Plancy, C. de, *Légendes des saintes images*, Paris, 1862.

Pomeroy, S., *Goddesses, Whores, Wives and Slaves*, New York, 1975.

Pourrat, H., *Histoire des gens dans les montagnes du centre*, Paris, 1959.

Preston, J. (ed.), *Mother Worship*, Chapel Hill, 1982.

Purce, J., *The Magic Spiral*, London, 1974.

Quispel, G., *The Secret Book of Revelation*, London, 1979.

Raeber, L., *Our Lady of the Hermits*, Einsiedeln, 1975.

Rákóczi, B., *The Painted Caravan*, The Hague, 1954.

Ravenscroft, T., *The Spear of Destiny*, London, 1973.

Rawson, P., *Tantra*, London, 1973.

Rawson, P., *The Art of Tantra*, London, 1973.

Reid, V., *Towards Aquarius*, London, 1969.

Renoud, G., *Notre-Dames, des Minimes à Montmerle*, Bourg, 1946.

Reynouard, J. and Sabatier, P., *Riom le Beau et ses Fleurons*, Clermont-Ferrand, 1973.

Ribón, A., 'Breve historia de la virgen de la Vega, patrona de Salamanca', *El Adelanto*, 30 August, 1981.

Riklin, F., *Jeanne d'Arc*, Zürich, 1972.

Rivière, J., *Saint-Savin en Lavedan*, Lourdes, 1982.

Robine, J., *Notre-Dame de la Garde*, Paris, 1978.

Robinson, J. (ed.), *The Nag Hammadi Library in English*, Leiden, 1977.

Ross Williamson, H., *Historical Whodunits*, London, 1955.

Rougemont, D. de, *Passion and Society*, London, 1940, revised and augmented 1956.

Rougier, M., *Notre-Dame de Paix à Picpus*, Paris, undated.

Roy, Y. *Le Testament des Templiers à Chinon*, Paris, 1974.

Runciman, S., *The Medieval Manichee*, Cambridge, 1947.

Saillens, E., *Nos Vierges Noires, leurs origines*, Paris, 1945.

Saintyves, P., *Les saints successeurs des dieux*, Paris, 1907.

Salvat, R., *Notre-Dame des Voirons*, Boège, 1981.

Sánchez-Pérez, J., *El Culto Mariano en España*, Madrid, 1943.

Sandars, N. (trans.), *The Epic of Gilgamesh*, Harmondsworth, 1960.

Saxer, V., *Le Culte de Marie-Madeleine en occident au Moyen Age*, Paris, 1959.

Schmitt, F., 'Vom Geheimnis der schwarzer Madonnen', *Königsteiner Jahrbuch*, Königstein i.Taurus, 1957.

Schnell, H., *Köln St Kolumba. Madonna in der Trümmern*, Munich, 1981.

Scholem, G., *On the Kabbalah and its Symbolism*, London, 1965.

Schonfield, H., *Secrets of the Dead Sea Scrolls*, London, 1956.

Schonfield, H., *The Essene Odyssey*, Shaftesbury, 1984.
Sède, G. de, *Les Templiers sont parmi nous*, Paris, 1962.
Sède, G. de, *Le Sang des Cathares*, Paris, 1966.
Sède G. de, *La Race fabuleuse*, Paris, 1973.
Sède G. de, *La Rose-Croix*, Paris, 1978.
Sèdir, *Les Rose-Croix*, Paris, 1953.
Sérénac, P., 'Les pouvoirs surnaturels des vierges noires', *Nostra*, 31 March 1983.
Seznec, J., *The Survival of the Pagan Gods*, New York, 1953.
Singer, J., *Androgyny, Toward a New Theory of Sexuality*, London, 1976.
Singer, (ed.), *The Jewish Encyclopedia*, London, 1901-6.
Sisters of St Thomas de Villeneuve, *La Vierge Noire de Paris*, Paris, 1982.
Smith, M., *The Secret Gospel*, London, 1975.
Smith, M., *Jesus the Magician*, London, 1978.
Sole, A., *La Mare de Déu del Claustre*, Solsona, 1966.
Stadler, J.-K., *Altötting Heilige Kapelle*, Munich, 1982.
Stewart, D., *The Foreigner. A Search for the First Century Jesus*, London, 1981.
Stone, M., *When God was a Woman*, London, 1976.
Stroud, J. and Thomas, G. (ed.), *Images of the Untouched*, Dallas, 1982.
Strub, M. and Moullet, M., *L'Eglise des Cordeliers de Fribourg*, Fribourg, undated.
Sykes, E., *Everyman's Dictionary of Non-Classical Mythology*, London, 1968.
Talbot, L. 'Sarah, la vierge noire des Saintes-Maries-de-le-Mer', *Atlantis*, no. 266, pp.169-79, January 1972.
Taylor, F., *The Alchemists*, London, 1951.
Thomas, P., *Notre Dame de Liesse*, Liesse, 1976.
Thompson, W., *The Time Falling Bodies Take to Light*, London, 1981.
Tournier, M., *The Four Wise Men*, London, 1982.
Toury, H., *Gerzat*, Clermont-Ferrand, 1964.
Toynbee, A. (ed.), *The Crucible of Christianity*, London, 1969.
Trible, P., *God and the Rhetoric of Sexuality*, Philadelphia, 1978.
Trompetto. M., *Storia del Santuario di Oropa*, Biella, 1979.
Turberville, A., *Medieval Heresy and the Inquisition*, London, 1920.
Ulanov, A., *The Feminine in Jungian Psychology and in Christian Theology*, Evanston, 1972.
Vacandard, E., *Vie de Saint Bernard*, Paris, 1895.
Vaes, H. and Schmitz, M., 'Le grand oeuvre de l'Abbaye d'Orval', *L'Action et les Arts Liturgiques*, nos 2 and 3, 1947.
Valléry-Radot, I., *Bernard de Fontaines*. Paris. 1963.

Vanderspeeten, H.-P., *Notre-Dame de la Consolation à Vilvorde*, Brussels, 1879.

Vazeille, A., *La Tour d'Auvergne et sa Région*, Clermont-Ferrand, 1977.

Verkest, I. and Coppens, C., *Het Eeuwfeest van Onze Lieve Vrouw van Affligem*, Affligem, 1946.

Vielva, M., 'La antigua abadía de Husillos (Palencia)', *Boletín de la Sociedad Castellana de Excursiones*, 1903, pp. 19-20.

Vigneron, C., *Grandes heures de l'histoire de Stenay*, Bar-le-Duc, 1978.

Villette, J., 'Que savons-nous de Notre-Dame de Chartres?', *Notre-Dame de Chartres*, no. 21, pp. 10-15, 1974.

Voragine, James of, *The Golden Legend*, ed. Ellis, London, 1900, 1255-1266.

Voragine, J. de, *La Légende de Sainte Marie Madeleine*, Paris, 1921.

Warner, M., *Alone of All Her Sex*, London, 1976.

Weston, J., *From Ritual to Romance*, London, 1920.

White, V., *Notes on Gnosticism*, London, 1969 (Guild of Pastoral Psychology Pamphlet no. 59).

Whitmont, E., *Return of the Goddess*, London, 1983.

Wilkins, E., *The Rose-Garden Game*, London, 1969.

Willems, J.-B., *O.L.V. van Affligem*, Brussels, 1924.

Wilson, E., *The Dead Sea Scrolls 1947-1969*, London, 1969.

Wilson, R. McL., *The Gnostic Problem*, London, 1958.

Wimet, P.-A., *Notre-Dame de Boulogne-sur-Mer*, Colmar, 1976.

Woodman, M., *Addiction to Perfection*, Toronto, 1982.

Yamauchi, E., *Pre-Christian Gnosticism*, London, 1973.

Yates, F. A., *Giordano Bruno and the Hermetic Tradition*, London, 1964.

Zingg, T., *Das Kleid der Einsiedler Muttergottes*, Einsiedeln, 1974.

Zuckerman, A., *A Jewish Princedom in Feudal France*, New York, 1972.

Index

Only references within the main text are given.

Liberia, 116
Libra, 138
Libyan Sibyl, 7
Liesse, 1, 32
Lila, 42
Lilaeus, 43
Lilith, 34–42, 44ff, 47, 87, 101, 122,
    127, 130, 131
Limoux, 58, 78, 80, 82, 101, 111,
    112, 145
Lincoln, H., 14
Lohengrin, 68, 110
Loire, 19, 118
Loki, 91
London, 63, 86
Longinus, 115
Longpont, 55, 64, 74, 104
Lorda, 39
Loreto, 1, 3, 25
Lorraine, 12, 111
Lorus, 40
Lotharingia, 83
Louis VII, 103
Louis IX, see Saints
Louis XI, 15, 21, 59, 68
Louis XIII, 111
Louis XIV, 110, 111
Lourdes, 28, 39, 40, 102, 134
Luc-sur-Aude, 78
Luc-sur-Mer, 78
Lucan of Cordoba, 81
Lucca, 105, 117 ff, 129
Lucera, 8, 68, 70
Lucian of Samosata, 76
Lucius, 62
Lucus, 63
Ludgdunum, 39
Lug, 60, 63, 77, 79, 83
Lupercalia, 55
Lycis, 52
Lygodesma, 54
Lyons, 18, 57 ff, 63, 70, 78, 79, 83,
    100, 149

Maat, 63, 131
Mabd, 85
Mabinogion, 87
Maccabees, 50, 60, 149
MacDonald, G., 35

Macha, 83, 85
Madrid, 58, 115
Magdala, 97, 98, 127
Magi, 7, 31
Mahram Bilqis, 34
Maia, 51, 70, 79
Maiesta, 51
Majorca, 107
Makeda, 31
Manda d'Hayye, 39
Mandaeans, 39, 124
Manfredonia, 56
Manosque, 10, 11, 71
Le Mans, 9
Mantinea, 69
Marceille, 111, 112
Mardoll, 92
Maria the Jewess/Prophetess, 35, 98,
    140
Marib, 34
Marie, F., 80, 81, 82
Marina, 122
Markale, J., 87, 129
Mars, 71, 72, 81, 83, 89, 119
Marsac, Girart de, 108
Marseilles, 17, 18, 20, 43, 44, 46, 54,
    55, 58, 60, 63, 70, 82, 86, 98, 99,
    100, 111, 119, 122, 123, 129, 145
Martilla, 98
Mary, Blessed Virgin, 6, 7, 12, 19, 20,
    39, 45, 53, 55, 61, 86, 93, 96, 116,
    117, 124, 128, 131, 139
Mary, Gospel of, 95
Mary Salome, 24, 98
Massilia, 54
Matronit, 37
Matthias, 149
Mauriac, 20, 58
Maxentius, 122
Maximian, Emperor, 115, 122
Maximinus, 98, 99, 123
Maya, 29, 131
Mayres, 117
Mazarin, Cardinal, 111, 112
Meaux, 65
Medea, 24
Mediterranean, 3, 18, 119
Medusa, 40, 47
Melchidezek, 23

INDEX